A
TASTE OF
PROVENCE
CAREY MORE &
JULIAN MORE

A TASTE OF
PROVENCE

CAREY MORE & JULIAN MORE

PAVILION
MICHAEL JOSEPH

FOR VISAN

First published in Great Britain in 1988 by
PAVILION BOOKS LIMITED
196 Shaftesbury Avenue, London WC2H 8JL
in association with Michael Joseph Limited
27 Wrights Lane, London W8 5TZ

Designed by Bernard Higton
Map by David Williams

British Library Cataloguing in Publication Data
More, Carey
A Taste of Provence.
1. Food : French dishes :
Provençal dishes – Recipes
I. Title   II. More, Julian,
641.5955'9

ISBN 1–85145–122–6 (Hardback)
ISBN 1–85145–313–X (Paperback)

Typeset by Wyvern Typesetting, Bristol
Colour originated by CLG, Verona, Italy

Printed and bound in Italy by New Interlitho, Milan

Published with the co-operation of l'Auberge de Provence,
41 Buckingham Gate, London SW1.   Tel: (01) 834 6655.

CONTENTS

Recipes compiled by Sheila More

Montélimar

Aiguebelle HONEY

LIQUEURS Valréas OLIVES •Rémuzat

Richerenches •Nyons LAMB

TRUFFLES •Visan GAME

4 WINE Vaison-la-Romaine MOUNTAIN
•Mondragon SAUSAGE

WINE 10 •Entrechaux

Séguret HERBS Sisteron

3 Malaucène WINE Mt. Ventoux 5

Beaumes de Venise •Sault Château
Arnoux

Châteauneuf GOAT'S CHEESE
du Pape •Carpentras NOUGAT •Banon

Tavel CRYSTALLISED FRUIT
ROSÉ
WINE St. Saturnin d'Apt

•Avignon 9

FRUIT 2 •Gargas 7
Chateaurenard •Cabrières Apt •Reillanne
VEGETABLES •Cavaillon 11 •Buoux •Céreste
•Bonnieux

SAUSAGE Les Alpilles
Baux Durance
•Arles

1 •
Camargue Lambesc •Rians
RICE RED WINE

•Aix-en-Provence
CALISSONS

FISH Marseilles WHITE WINE
•6 •Cassis
Le Ciotat RED WINE
•Bandol

MEDITERRANEAN SEA

RESTAURANTS

1. Le Moulin de Tante Yvonne   17
2. Bistrot à Michel   13/14 64
3. Domaine de la Cabasse   16
4. La Beaugravière   17
5. La Bonne Etape   12 Gleize 38
6. Chez Aldo   28 56
7. L'Auberge de Reillanne   13
8. L'Oustau de Baumanière 18
9. St. Hubert (St. Saturnin d'Apt) 10
10. St. Hubert (Entrechaux)

46 Avignon

Nostradamus, that Provençal medic, astronomer and prophet, a man of normally frugal habits, reports from sixteenth-century St-Rémy:

At this legendary supper the guests, after washing their hands with rose water, consumed at least fifteen courses: pine nut and marzipan tart, commonly known as mortar bread, with sugar, rose water, and almonds; fresh asparagus; heart, liver, and crop of wild birds; roast buckskin; calves' and heifers' heads, boiled in their skins; capons, hens, pigeons, with tongue, ham, and lemon sauce; a whole roast kid each, served on a square silver plate, with the juice of sour cherries; turtle-doves, partridges, pheasants, quails, cranes, pipits, and other winged creatures gently and carefully roasted; olives from Salon as accompaniment; a cock cooked in sugar and rose water, served to each of the guests on a little silver platter; then a piglet each; a roast peacock in a white, or rather rust-coloured sauce, made of livers and a delicious aromatic concoction which the Spaniards call 'garronchos'; quinces with sugar, cloves and cinnamon; artichoke hearts; and finally, hands washed again, many and varied sorts of sweetmeats of coriander, Florentine fennel, almond, candied cloves, orange-peel, cinnamon, all scented with musk.

A TASTE OF PROVENCE

Four centuries after Nostradamus, I attended a wedding dinner.

As an aperitif we were served champagne on the lawn. The first course, *Salade folle au saumon fumé*, contained smoked salmon. Nothing very Provençal so far. But there was an excuse: the bridegroom was born in Champagne, the bride in England.

Things got more authentic. Next there was *Filet de loup grillé au fenouil*, sea bass grilled with fennel, accompanied by a dry, flinty Côtes-du-Rhône white from Domaine St-Claude. After that came the *Trou Provençal*, a traditional pause between fish and meat with a sorbet of *marc de Provence*, that powerful 70° brandy made with pips, stalks

Near Buisson

and skins of crushed grapes. Then, suddenly, the Grand March from *Aïda* boomed nobly into the night, while a whole flaming lamb was carried in procession around the guests. This was *Agneau du Ventoux flambé avec ses légumes*, lamb raised on the herbs of Mont Ventoux, flamed in brandy, with a *tian* (Provençal for *gratin*) of aubergines; instead of the heavy red wine which suits lamb in winter – Châteauneuf-du-Pape or Gigondas – the warmer weather called for a light country wine of the Principality of Orange, also from Domaine St-Claude. Then back to champagne for the *Pièce Montée*, an elaborate guitar-shaped cake, and *Salade de fruits*.

At Visan, where high days are really high, this menu was considered light fare by some hardened wedding-goers. But, like other celebrations, Carey More's wedding to Philippe Manoeuvre was a good excuse to get legs under the table, and enjoy the pleasure of a sit-down meal with friends and family. Which is what we love in Provence: at long outdoor tables after the Visan wine festival, sharing a *Grand Aïoli* – a classic combination of poached salt cod, boiled lamb, vegetables (carrots, celery, chick-peas, cauliflower), snails and hard-boiled eggs served with the famous mayonnaise ('aï' with 'oli', garlic with olive oil in Provençal); or in winter, long indoor tables where whole families foregather for Sunday lunch at the St-Hubert Restaurant in Entrechaux, ninety-year-olds enjoying their wild boar or pheasant, nine-

month-old babies, their faces joyously smeared with *Oeufs à la neige*.

The creation of this book is inspired by those Provençal family binges; for its creators are a Provençal family – albeit adoptive. The olive trees and English lawn in front of our farmhouse seem to symbolize a fortuitous combining of roots; over the years, the trees have begun to bear olives and the grass has become, if not exactly nail-clip-pered, more lawnlike. Carey, who took the photographs, and Sheila, who prepared the recipes, cook for pleasure, not professionally. And I am a food-lover, not a food-writer. Our home is here, and some of the best Provençal gastronomy is home cooking. Recipes are comparatively sim-ple and within our own capabilities, with ingredients mostly accessible in the Home Coun-ties and Connecticut; occasionally we take a flyer with a challenging recipe from the pros – chefs and culinary wizards who have revealed their secrets and who, with the generosity of cooks, allowed us to borrow them.

As its title suggests, this is a taster rather than any attempt at a definitive work. Over the years, Escoffier, Reboul, and Elizabeth David have already done that; to the last I owe a debt of gratitude for starting me off as a Sunday cook, enthusiastically plugging my 3oz cubes of lamb with bacon, rolled in chopped garlic and parsley for a *Daube à l'avignonnaise*.

Our own search for the true taste of Provence

Guarding the olives

La Bonne Etape restaurant.

has taken us beyond Avignon – south to the coast, Marseilles, Cassis and Bandol; east via the Lubéron, rich in good restaurants, to the wonders of Gleize *père et fils* at Château-Arnoux. An easy day's outing, at most; more often, an hour or so from home. Purposely we have not attempted too much; the cuisine east of the Durance (and particularly Nice) deserves a book to itself.

Provençal cooking, at its best, is one of the world's most healthy and balanced. Its particular ingredients are garlic, olive oil, and herbs, known for their therapeutic qualities. Garlic against cancer; olive oil against heart and liver diseases; and herbs, according to Maurice Messegué, for practically every ailment – sage for diabetes, savory for impotence, lavender for stomach cramps.

Perhaps it is the subtle use of herbs in the Gleizes' cooking that makes their restaurant, La Bonne Etape, one of the most celebrated in Provence. From father Pierre to son Jany the regional

secrets of Jean Giono's 'country of light' have been passed on with a brilliant lightness of touch.

With a little help, too, from a maternal grandmother. In her kitchen, Jany, aged five, stood on a vegetable box, eyes only just level with the table, and cooked chicken livers. 'After a walk in the garrigue,' he told me, 'with all those intoxicating aromatic smells titillating your nostrils, you don't come home and cook a chicken in cream.'

Hence, at La Bonne Etape, you will find steak with rosemary, duck with lavender honey, rabbit with hyssop, salad with purslane (a weed to most of us!), *petits gris* (Provençal snails) with fennel and thyme. For pungent stuffings in ravioli, for courgette flowers in highly-flavoured tomato sauce, and other inventive exotica, there is basil, parsley, tarragon, oregano, chives, savory and wild thyme. All from the hotel garden or local growers.

During the past thirty years, Pierre Gleize has built up his network of Haute-Provence suppliers,

L'assiette des desserts,
L'Auberge de Reillanne

and his ingredients radiate sunlight and fresh-ness: pigeons fed on local corn, wheat, and lentils; Sisteron lamb, Banon goat's cheese, and olive oil from down the road.

Olive oil, of all ingredients, puts the Mediter-ranean stamp on Provençal cooking. The Mediterranean's Muslim and Christian countries share the symbolism of oil as an unction of bene-diction. The Koran speaks of the olive tree as 'a blessed tree neither of the East nor West'.

From the centenarians of Asia minor, where garlic is supposed to have originated, to our senior citizens of Visan, spritely at their games of *boules*, that reeker of the warm south has helped keep the blood circulating and the heart youthful. For those who like garlic bread but not garlic breath, let me recommend three grains of coffee chewed after the *aïoli*. Or a sprig of parsley from your herb garden.

Almost every fresh ingredient for the best French country cooking seems to be magicked out of the strong Provençal earth. 'Let's not be chauvinistic,' said Pierre Gleize, 'but beef, butter and cream are practically the only things I get from elsewhere.'

These classic ingredients of Gallic cuisine are naturally used in Provençal cooking too, but with a lighter touch. It's all in the fine art of balance. At L'Auberge de Reillanne, Marie-Anne Founès cooked me four gastronomic meals over two days, with delicate use of cream, butter, and wine, and

my liver gave not a twinge. Whereas I have felt bilious after one dollop of industrialized supermarket mayonnaise.

The supermarket fast-food mentality naturally upsets gastronomes, but not for the more obvious reasons; Provençal supermarkets can be as good as anywhere. Restaurateurs see it as a sociological as much as an alimentary problem. '*Télé* dinners and *le Fast Food* mean a loss of human contact. Leisurely eating together is a primordial rite,' said Michel Bosc, owner and chef of Bistrot à Michel,

*Statue of poet
Frédéric Mistral, Arles*

dishes required little preparation, ingredients just thrown into a stewpot for slow cooking while the family was working in the fields; others were much more finicky. Michel's grandmother used to spend hours on her *fricot d'épinards*, preparing clams and spinach for intricate stuffing. But basically, this is a country cuisine, often frugal, with most of its traditional dishes having peasant origins – what was available in the neighbourhood (game in the forest, fish on the coast, herbs, mushrooms, truffles), or on your land (lamb, figs, almonds, olives, honey), what you could barter (wine for corn), or preserve in the attic for winter (dried fruits, beans, sausage and cured ham hanging from the rafters). 'Psychologically,' Michel said, 'the knowledge that the year's cycle would, weather permitting, deliver the goods, well, that kept the spirits up. The fruits of the earth return. They are always there – even dormant in winter.'

Winter starts late, sometimes not till after Christmas, and often dramatically. It is short and sharp, and a sudden violent drop in temperature can devastate olive trees. Eighty per cent were lost in the great freeze-up of 1985. But the cycle of the four seasons appealed to Marie-Anne Founès, Parisian journalist-turned-chef, who with her husband Florent converted a medieval Templers' Hospice of the Middle Ages into a friendly country hotel and restaurant, patronized by Henri Cartier-Bresson and the King and Queen of Belgium. 'We

the village bar at Cabrières d'Avignon, meeting place of local workmen and eating place of the summer trendies of nearby Gordes. Surrounded by nostalgic movie posters of Pagnol's *Fanny* and *Marius*, Michel continued: 'You are what you eat. Myself, I eat for pleasure, gourmand rather than gourmet. I've never had health trouble. It's all in the mind – feeling guilty about having a good time.'

Son of an Avignon baker, Michel believes that the lost art of Provençal home-cooking is being rediscovered and developed by a whole new generation of chefs. In their grandmothers' day, some

Visan in autumn

Michel Bosc, Le Bistrot à Michel

chose Provence because of the perpetual, astonishing changes of light – and the seasonal produce that goes with them. You feel close to nature, there's something different for the kitchen every week, and I change the menu with what I can get. Take dried herbs: their perfume is quite different from fresh. Same with garlic. In winter I make the soup *Aïgo-boulido* with dried garlic and sage. It wouldn't taste the same in June.'

The romance of Provence can trap us outsiders into a somewhat rose-tinted view. Marie-Anne waxed lyrical about Sisteron lambs being nourished on the natural vitamins in savory, which apparently they can sniff out in the fields. But for many years now, Provence has had to adapt to a flight from artisanal peasant-style farming to the industrialized agriculture of the Rhône Valley. Also, many of the upland villages and towns would be in a bad way without tourism. And so would the restaurants. Yet with it inevitably comes the regimentation of package-tour mentality. Even as I was enjoying Marie-Anne's pigeon salad – slices of warm pigeon and baked pear on a bed of crisp lettuce – a German food-writer commented loudly from the next table: 'We Germans will not tolerate errors of translation on the menu!'

The Latour sisters of La Domaine de Cabasse, a hotel-restaurant on their wine property at Séguret, also bemoaned the more idiotic aspects of standardization: 'For many years, *Michelin* would not put us in their guide because we refused to have a front desk. This is our home, that's its charm, and we don't want it looking like a Novotel!' Nadine, the cook, was equally emphatic about the role of Provençal food and wine: 'Of course, I adapt it to what foreigners like to some extent. Even vegetarians. But I've got my locals to feed, and they don't want to pay good money for a meal they can cook at home. There's plenty of money about in Vaucluse, and I must give value for it. On Sunday, they want to be surprised – by something like my *Feuilleté de truite aux épinards* (flaky pastry with trout and spinach) or *Perdreaux aux lentilles* (partridge with lentils).'

Such evolution has been going on since the

Port of Cassis

famous Trois Frères Provençaux opened their Paris restaurant in 1789, and is the pride of many other fine cooks celebrated in this book.

At Le Moulin de Tante Yvonne, Lambesc, 81-year-old Yvonne Soliva does the cooking with only one kitchen help, while her husband, André, takes the orders sitting at our table. Their former olive oil mill is more like a private home than a restaurant. Even more so for us because of the Visan wines: Madame Soliva was 1981's Queen of the Visan Wine Festival, and has served its wines in her restaurant ever since.

More unusual still is the highly individualistic ex-liner steward, Max Veron, who would only do a *Bouillabaisse* for us, if we swore not to reveal the address of his Marseilles restaurant. Publicity? *Merci, non!* He had his clientele of regulars and that was good enough for him.

And the young turks of the trade: Charles Mouret at Entrechaux, Guy Jullien at Mondragon, and Jean-André Charial at Les Baux. All three are at very different stages of evolution. Monsieur Mouret's St-Hubert still has a very local feel about it, providing excellent game in honour of the patron saint of hunters; Monsieur Jullien's La Beaugravière, formerly a dreary commercial hotel on the N7, has begun to attract food lovers from far and wide with its truffle specialities and particularly good wine list; and L'Oustau de Baumanière, where Monsieur Charial commands the kitchen, is a world-famous temple of gastronomy which demands none of that stuffy, fat-cat reverence too often associated with such places.

Some of our favourite restaurants and recipes appear in this book, but they are only part of a larger picture of the cuisine of Provence. There are also visits to mountain sheep farmers, truffle markets, honey-purveyors to Fortnum & Mason, and distilling monks. There is a wild hunting picnic (with cabaret by the hunters), and lavish lunches with winemakers. Not to mention a great cook no one has ever heard of – the late Madame Campdorasse. For several years in the Sixties, whenever we could escape to Grimaud, she

Sisteron Lamb at La Bonne Étape

cooked for us: wonderful meals which made us aware of this southern cuisine for the first time. I shall never forget her sturdy, determined shape charging into the garden in search of *mesclun*, that Midi salad mixture of dandelions, lamb's-lettuce and wild chicory.

Madame Campdorasse was Majorquin in origin. So many Provençals, like their language, originated somewhere else. And their cuisine has benefited by an eclectic injection of new influences. The Greeks brought the vine, the Romans the olive tree. In more recent times came the Italians with pasta, the Spaniards with red peppers and paella, and North African *pieds noirs* and Arabs with couscous. The Arabs also, of course, brought mint tea, while we English have regrettably only contributed mint sauce. When we give lunch to our French neighbours,

nowadays they find no leg of lamb complete without it – followed by *crumble aux pommes*.

Long summer lunches in the shade of our grape-vine *tonnelle*, raising a lazy hand to pick a grape or even a bunch, listening to the soporific song of cicadas as conversation slows to a pleasant susurration and the heat-haze hangs heavy over Visan village, these are the stuff Midi afternoons are made of – until the sweet, inevitable crash-out.

Not as spectacular as the terrace of L'Oustau de Baumanière, perhaps. What can rival the view of Les Baux above, ruins perched on stark grey rock, scent of *garrigue* and *haute cuisine*, tinkling satyr's head fountain, and cypresses swaying in a not-so-light wind? 'This, Mildred, is not a breeze,' an American lady at the next table informed her friend. 'It's a mistral.'

It takes lamb as good as the *Gigot d'agneau en croûte* and a terrace as beautiful to drag us away from ours. Some of the most rewarding dishes, with the least pretensions, have been our own experiments with the seemingly limitless ingredients this soil and sea provide. Almost all those mentioned are 'made in Provence'. And there is no French perfume more exotic than the smoke of a fire of vinestocks, mingling with the aroma of wine, garlic, olive, herbs, and orange peel, which wafts from the *daube* in one's own oven. It is beyond price, or the talents of all the alchemists of Grasse. And it is distilled at home.

Cassis

THE MAGIC HOUR

*. . . . down there at the far end of the monastery
behind the glowing-red windows of the distillery, you would
hear Father Gaucher singing at the top of his voice. . . .*
ALPHONSE DAUDET, 'FATHER GAUCHER'S ELIXIR'

There are few things more delightful, during that magic hour before a Midi sunset, than partaking of a cocktail mixed by a Trappist monk.

Brother Gérard clearly enjoyed this moment of release from his vow of silence. In the tasting room of the abbey of Notre Dame d'Aiguebelle, where he is in charge of production, the dash and flair of his concocting rivalled a Riviera barman's: gin, passion fruit liqueur, peach and apricot juice, with just a hint of raspberry brandy. 'It passes the test,' he murmured after a connoisseur's swig, and handed me my glass. I said a brief prayer for a safe drive home.

Monfrin

Father Gérard in the distillery

Founded in 1137, the abbey of Aiguebelle was celebrating eight and a half centuries of prayer, study, hard work and hangovers. In the 1880s Père Jean, the abbey's veterinary surgeon, discovered an elixir which cured the animals; in 1937 the forgotten recipe was revived and became the famous Aiguebelle liqueur. During the Second World War, the monks hid, clothed, and fed members of the American Forces; after the war, short of sugar for the distillery, Aiguebelle received regular supplies from grateful Trappist monasteries in the States – and was thus back in business before their competitors, Chartreuse and Benedictine, had even got their alambics lit.

Aiguebelle also produces (among many aperitifs of local herbs, fruit and nuts) *Crème de Myrtilles*. This does for rosé wine what *Crème de Cassis* does for white wine in a Kir. Except that the added fruity taste is tart bilberry rather than sweet blackcurrant. A dash in the bottom of the glass, topped up with chilled rosé (or red, if you prefer), and you have a Myro.

Myro was originally a shepherd's drink. During the autumn 'transhumance', bringing his herd down from mountain pastures, he would collect a

Abbey of Notre Dame, Aiguebelle

Nyons

Near Vaison-la-Romaine

supply of ripe bilberries. Crushed and mixed with the year's new rosé wine, the bilberries made a refreshing drink, said to improve night vision. Ideal for coming down Mont Ventoux on a moonless night. In fact a low-priced but full-bodied Côtes-du-Ventoux rosé is best for making a Myro; keep the grander Tavel to drink straight.

Cool reds also make a pleasant summer *apéro*. I even caught a distinguished maker of our region's grandest wine, Châteauneuf-du-Pape, taking a bottle of his youngest red from the fridge with no shame whatsoever. But it's better – and a lot cheaper – to stick to lighter reds: *vins du pays* and table wines. They shouldn't be drunk much colder than 14°C. Cool, rather than iced. Three methods work: put just the bottom of a bottle on ice, rather than encasing it; ice up a decanter before putting the wine in; or put the bottle in the bottom of the fridge – never in the freezer – and never for too long. It kills the wine.

But, for the locals born and bred, the only *apéro* is pastis, mother's milk of Provence. Its father was Monsieur Pernod, who commercialized absinthe, its more debilitating antecedent, in 1797. Having done its worst for Oscar Wilde, de Musset, and others, absinthe was banned in 1915. It was not till 1938 that its style of drink made a comeback in the Marseilles area, where dealing in such aromatics as aniseed and stronger stuff had always been part of the folklore. But the new drink called pastis was 'soft', not containing the dangerous

Tourte d'olives

plant absinthe, and quickly became France's most popular aperitif.

It is not difficult to home brew: pastis is made by mixing pure alcohol with essence of aniseed; it is steeped for a couple of days in powdered liquorice; then filtered and sugared to taste. Caterers for Marseilles weddings, by the way, have to provide four times the normal amount of pastis – and it all gets drunk.

Pastis is relatively sweet, and sweet aperitifs are popular in hot climates. It seems paradoxical to the English, used to port after dinner and sweet wines with the dessert. But here in Provence, sweet aperitifs served cool not only refresh but restore energy, expended in the heat, with their high natural sugar content. Our strong, golden

bread, spread *tapénade*, a black olive paste, or *boutargue*, 'caviar' of grey mullet's roe.

These are served at the magic hour of sunset, which is always earlier in the south, the light changing every minute, providing a feast for the eye as well as the stomach. We like to make the most of it. So we spin it out, sometimes with quite unexpected dishes like hot aubergine and goat's cheese with cinnamon (*Chèvre à l'aubergine*), to be spread on toasted bread like *tapénade*. Everyday aperitif treats on our terrace are thinly-sliced mountain sausage from Vaison-la-Romaine market, radishes, and our staple black olives from Nyons.

Nyons olives are reckoned to be among the best in France. While restaurateur Yvonne Soliva lovingly massaged a chicken with olive oil before roasting, she told me: 'The best oil comes from Maussane nowadays. The olives are half ripe and they are pressed only once. But the best black eating olives are still from Nyons.'

The Ramade olive oil mill at Nyons has been in the family for four generations. Ramade's boutique is housed around the nineteenth-century olive press (still operating) which is used as display shelves for other artisanal products – soap, olive wood kitchen utensils, honey, olive oil (bottles aromatized differently for meat or fish grills, or sprinkling on pizza). There are two huge bins of black olives – natural in water and sea-salt, or with *herbes de Provence*.

vins doux naturels from Rasteau and Beaumes-de-Venise refresh the sweet-toothed, and can be pleasantly addictive. One summer guest insisted on drinking Rasteau aperitif right through the meal, and had a head to prove it the next day.

Before the meal, Provençal *apéros* are always accompanied by something to eat. The habit reflects the Mediterranean influence of Middle Eastern *mezze* and Spanish *tapas*. Special occasions call for quite substantial things like *anchoïade* (anchovy paste with crushed garlic and olive oil). This accompanies *crudités*, such as raw carrots, cauliflower, celery, peppers, baby tomatoes, whatever is in season. Equally serve these with *aïoli* (recipe in Chapter 4). Anchovy puffs and mussel fritters are served hot. And on hot grilled

Ancient olive trees, St-Romain-en-Viennois

BEIGNETS DE MOULES

These mussel fritters are the recipe of Max Veron, owner of 'Chez Aldo' in a little-known fisherman's calanque near Marseilles. Serves 8–10 as appetizers.

3½oz/100g (¾ cup) sifted flour
2tbs/30ml olive oil
pinch salt
1 egg yolk
8fl oz/200ml (1 cup) water
1 egg white, stiffly beaten
2½oz/75g chopped mussels, or other fish

Mix together flour, oil, salt, egg yolk and water to a smooth cream. Fold in egg white and fish, and deep fry, by the spoonful. Serve finger-searing hot – with cocktail sticks.

Instead of fish, you can use chopped ham and cheese.

CHÈVRE À L'AUBERGINE

Goat's cheese and aubergine (eggplant) with cinnamon. Recipe of Madame Dijour of Faucon. This is her version of a pied noir dish, brought to Provence from Tunisia. Hence the use of cinnamon. We serve it on toast with aperitifs, but it also makes an excellent vegetable dish for 4–6 people.

2 medium aubergines (eggplants)
juice of 1 lemon
2 cloves garlic, crushed
salt
2 tbs/30ml olive oil
2–3 goat's cheeses, not too hard
1 tbs/15ml powdered cinnamon

Slice the aubergine (eggplant) but do not peel. Salt and leave to drain 1 hour. Dry. Put in large pan with olive oil, lemon juice and garlic. Cover and leave on very low heat to soften, stirring occasionally. This way they will not need more oil. Break up the cheeses and crumble into the aubergines (eggplants), add the cinnamon and mix well. You probably won't need salt.

Put in oven dish and cook for 20–30 minutes in pre-heated, moderate oven, 375°F/190°C/Gas Mark 5. Spread thickly on bread or toast and serve as an appetizer.

Chèvre à l'aubergine

TAPÉNADE

VG Delicious

Invention of Monsieur Meynier of Marseilles, about 100 years ago. The name comes from tapéno, *Provençal for capers, an essential ingredient often left out. This amount will last you a long time as it is deliciously potent. Store covered in the fridge. It keeps for several weeks.*

9oz/250g (1½ cups) stoned black (pitted ripe) olives
3½oz/100g canned anchovy fillets, drained
3½oz/100g canned tuna fish, drained
3½oz/100g (½ cup) capers, drained
sprig thyme
1 bay leaf crumbled
2 large cloves garlic, peeled
1 small glass brandy (optional)
4 tbs/60ml olive oil
black pepper to taste

Rinse all ingredients

Purée all ingredients except olive oil and seasoning in blender or food processor. With machine running slowly, pour in olive oil. Season with pepper – no salt. Serve at room temperature on bread or toast. Or with raw vegetables (celery, cauliflower florets, carrots, etc). Or as stuffing for hard-boiled (hard-cooked) eggs (mash yolks, mix with paste, and fill whites with mixture).

Or make Madame Latour's *Caviare d'aubergine*: bake an aubergine in its skin until soft, lift out the flesh and blend it with a little *tapénade* and olive oil. Delicious spread on grilled bread.

TRUFFLES AND OTHER STARTERS

He who gives up olive oil gives up his good taste.
PROVENÇAL PROVERB

The best way to eat a truffle,' said Madame Dijour, puffing on her pipe in the eloquent pause, 'is like a potato.' Not for nothing does Dijour – a close friend, though her first name is still a mystery – come from the land of caviar, serving in her childhood as a Soviet naval cadet. Now, in her very game seventies, she grows the world's second luxury comestible in an oak plantation round her beautiful old farmhouse near Faucon.

With a sardonic chuckle, she continued: 'It's basically a peasant dish – like all the best truffle dishes. You just chop up an onion and carrot,

View from Mont Ventoux

Poachers keep out!

sauté, add a little white wine, cook your truffle whole and unpeeled in the mixture, cut it in half and eat.'

I asked her if truffle-farmers themselves got rich feeding the rich. It was a high-risk business, Dijour assured me. A truffle's symbiosis was as capricious as its taste was subtle. Fifteen years from acorn to truffle-bearing oak, then only some may have the necessary short, horizontal roots on which truffles can grow. In June, pinhead-size truffles detach themselves from the root and begin their own lives. They need a hot, humid summer. 'Three lousy summers we've had. Either too dry, or too cool without rain,' said Dijour. 'In 1986, a colleague blamed Chernobyl. But I said, no, it's the weather and probably just as well. Who needs to die from a radioactive truffle? Such an expensive death!'

The black truffles of Vaucluse, either wild from the heavily guarded allotments on Mont Ventoux or from plantations like Dijour's, ripen only after the first frost, and it's then the fun or fuming begins. Tell it not in Périgord, but Provence now secretly supplements that over-reputed region's truffle production – as anyone prepared to brave the Carpentras truffle market at eight a.m. on a cold February morning can, at risk of life and limb, discover. 'We do the work,' said a Vaucluse dealer in astrakhan hat and fur-lined leather jacket, 'and Périgord gets the credit.'

The scene outside the Hotel l'Univers in the centre of Carpentras was a jollier version of arms-dealing in downtown Sofia or dope-dealing in up-country Colombia. A youth in dark glasses hot footing from the slopes of Mont Ventoux flashed open his plastic shopping bag to a scornful woman in a black fedora; she weighed out a few truffles and, after some haggling, gave the boy Fr2500; by the time his truffles reached Paris, they would be worth Fr7000. The next deal, the seller didn't trust Fedora's scales, insisting they reweigh on his own. '*Elle n'est pas commode*,' he confided to me afterwards. 'She's a pain.'

There is deep suspicion of outsiders. Glares and grunts greeted me wherever I went, on the grounds that I might be a tax inspector's spy. Deals are strictly cash and undeclared, for complex reasons traditional in the truffle business. Some people don't have licences to deal, and pay very heavy fines if caught. Jean-Claude Dumas, a legit buyer who had just rescued me from having my tape-recorder smashed, whispered: 'The real

Truffle dealers,
Richerenches bar

heavy deals are done across the street – in the carpark.' And he disappeared, dodging the rush-hour traffic of Place Aristide Briant, with a word of warning on no account to follow.

It seemed a hell of a hassle for an *Omelette aux truffes*.

'I always get my truffles direct from the same grower in Richerenches. They are the best in our region,' said Guy Jullien, brandishing a big preserving jar full of the black gold deep-frozen, wrapped in foil. We had just swooned over his *Omelette aux truffes*, an all-year-round speciality of La Beaugravière, Mondragon. 'Nothing preserves as well as freezing truffles: they keep all of their subtle natural flavour.'

Monsieur Ollivier of Richerenches explained the secret of the area's truffle yield: 'Soil which filters water. A flood on a *truffier* finishes it off – and you've seen how heavy our rain can be!' His sheepdog, Plume, was snuffling about under the oaks. Nose down meant a find. His front paws scrabbled, and out came a truffle under his back

legs like a ball from a rugby scrum. 'Their size can be anything from a grain of pepper to a Cavaillon melon.'

Back at the Ollivier farmhouse, Madame Ollivier revealed a few of her truffle tips: put the sliced truffle in the omelette mixture overnight; use chicory in a *Salade Rothschild* (she didn't call it that, though it's the name on the menu!) rather than lettuce – it goes better with the taste of truffle; bake a whole truffle in flaky pastry.

There the secrets stopped. When it came to the excellent Ollivier pâté, made with pork, truffles and herbs, they were not giving too much away. Nor was the butcher who specialized in the renowned *saucisson d'Arles*: when I rang him to enquire what gave it that deliciously spicy taste (*Larousse* says they use some horsemeat), he hung up on me. But this much I did learn from the Olliviers: a pig killed that morning had become

Salade Rothschild

Near Séderon

the pâté I was now eating, and had just the fresh, earthy quality I would expect from a truffle-farmer's pâté. 'It's crazy to be dependent just on truffles for a living,' said Monsieur Ollivier. 'Have some more pâté!'.

The best known of our pâtés, of course, is *pâté de grives*. But somehow pâté does not seem the right place for a thrush. Perhaps I am over-sensitive; Provençal hunters, mocked by Stendhal for their trigger-happy shooting habits, also count finches, young magpies, and starlings as pâté-worthy. I have only tasted the thrush version, which owes its specially delicate perfume to the juniper berries, grapes and corn of the thrush's diet in these parts. But I still prefer the gamier taste of *pâté de marcassin* — young wild boar. Equally good made with pheasant.

Although the St-Hubert is a game restaurant in winter, its best summer starter is *Sardine crue*, and

for anyone turned off by the idea of raw fish, let them just try Charles Mouret's sardines. I guarantee instant conversion.

We discovered a less controversial fish starter at another St-Hubert (at St-Saturnin d'Apt). Its spectacular terrace overlooking the Lubéron is a surprise after the entrance, an ordinary village house front door straight off the street. Beneath a clear blue sky with wispy white clouds, the sensual brown velvet of the mountain lay there like a sun-tanned nude — competition for Claude Arnaud's equally seductive *Brouillade d'oursin*. The coral contents of four half sea-urchins were mixed with lightly scrambled eggs, put back in their spiny black shells, and topped with chives and sweet peppers. This was one of the very rare occasions when Provence's self sufficiency let us down: the sea-urchins, Monsieur Arnaud admitted, came overnight by refrigerator express from the English Channel at Boulogne-sur-Mer! 'And special delivery to the door, too,' he added. 'For Mediterranean fish, I'd have to drive an hour to Avignon. I just haven't got the time. Distribution's gone crazy in France.'

No distribution problems for Pierre Gleize, though. All his produce comes direct to him at La Bonne Etape — including Mediterranean fish. But although wise eaters make a point of timing their journey on the Route Napoléon for a stop at Château-Arnoux, midway between Nice and Grenoble, they will not find sole, turbot, sea bass

Near Ménerbes

or red mullet on the menu. 'Fashionable fish are more expensive than they're worth,' commented Pierre, somewhat surprisingly for the owner of a restaurant of such prestige.

In these days of star chefs like Pierre and Jany Gleize, jetting about the world to educate would-be gastronomes in Hong Kong and Miami, Pierre Gleize is a refreshingly unaffected person. Born within half an hour of Château-Arnoux in the wild valley of the Jabron, he was destined to be a notary. To the fury of his parents, he became a pastrycook. A happy motorbike breakdown outside this former eighteenth-century staging post, then a railway station hotel, led Pierre to marry the owner's daughter, Arlette, and to rename the place La Bonne Etape – The Good Stopover. Each week his mother-in-law would show Pierre a new Provençal dish; and now Pierre, Jany, and Arlette have developed a simple inn into one of France's best and least pompous regional hotel–restaurants.

Regional is precisely the word. Even as Pierre welcomed us with a glass of champagne (his only non-regional wine), one of his suppliers came into the bar with a huge basket of *cèpes* for the kitchen. No nonsense of a tradesmen's entrance, everything splendidly informal in the Provençal manner. The mushroom man drank champagne with us.

We lunched memorably in the tapestried dining room overlooking a lakeside garden. It lasted from midday to 7.30, if not actually eating and drinking, talking about eating and drinking all that time.

And most memorable were the starters. The little masterpieces came one after another for a special tasting. The mushroom man's *cèpes* had been transformed into the stuffing for some extraordinary ravioli. Only the most inventive cooks would brave mixing orange with fish, as in the fish gâteau of *mostelle*, a delicate Mediterranean whiting accompanied by an orange butter. Then baby squid stuffed with green herbs and pine kernels. And the crowning glory visually and gastronomically – *fleurs de courgettes farcies sauce pomme d'amour*. These fig-like shapes are courgette blossoms stuffed with a subtle blend of vegetables, in a tomato sauce flavoured with coriander, chervil and basil. A stylish blend of yellow, green and pink on the plate, which made one hesitate before desecrating it with a greedy fork.

Anyone overdoing it at such a very good stopover as La Bonne Etape should take comfort in a simpler starter called *Aïgo-boulido*. Translated literally as Boiled Water, this recuperative garlic soup is in fact a winter favourite of two chefs, Nadine Latour and Marie-Anne Founès. It is reputed to revive one after a gastronomic orgy, influenza or an operation.

Or if you prefer your garlic less liquid, start the meal with pasta and *pistou*, that lively garlic-and-basil sauce which came to Provence from

Pierre and Jany Gleize tasting
Vacqueyras wine, La Bonne Etape

Oppedette

goule – violet artichoke hearts lightly cooked in a *mirepoix* (sautéed onions, carrots, celery and ham) with thyme and spices; Nadine Latour often does rice with pine kernels and raisins; and Dijour, when not cooking truffles like potatoes, makes a splendidly simple starter which she just calls Spiced Mushrooms.

As I write this, that perilous autumn mushroom season is upon us again. A tip from Lili Ramour, our neighbour: best to start mushrooming with experts, like a friend of ours with whom, during one afternoon's mushrooming in a Var forest, we found twenty-four non-poisonous varieties.

Sheila and Lili have just returned from the much-mushroomed Visan pinewoods with a sizeable haul of *lactaires*, *chanterelles*, and *trompettes de la mort*. Yes, the Trumpets of Death are quite safe – and delicious. Tonight we will have a much cheaper starter than truffles.

neighbouring Italy. For the pasta, we are lucky enough to get fresh noodles from a genuine Italian grocery in Vaison-la-Romaine; it is always worth seeking out the real thing – packet pasta just never tastes the same at all.

The North African influence in starters can be tasted at a charming and very reasonably-priced restaurant in Avignon, named after the Café des Nattes at Sidi Bou Said, Tunisia. Peppers with an onion relish are the components of their Salade Mechouïa. French cooks welcome the oriental influence in Provençal starters: Michel Bosc uses cummin and coriander in his *Artichauts à la bari-*

LACTAIRES
(LACTARIUS DELICIOSUS)

This recipe for wild mushrooms is from Madame Ramour of Visan. You can also use ordinary commercial white mushrooms, or bottled French ones. Serves 4.

1lb/450g fresh mushrooms
squeezed lemon juice
2 tsp/10 ml olive oil
2 tsp/10 ml white wine or wine vinegar
2 or 3 cloves garlic, crushed
handful chopped parsley
pinch grated nutmeg
black pepper
salt (optional)

Clean mushrooms under running tap, rinse in water containing lemon juice, and cut into equal pieces. Put the olive oil, white wine or vinegar into a frying pan (skillet) over a medium heat. Add the mushrooms, garlic, parsley, pepper and nutmeg. Cook, turning often, until the mushrooms have given up their moisture. Salt if necessary.

Serve immediately, either on their own with wholemeal (whole-wheat) bread and butter, or as an accompaniment to a roast or grilled (broiled) dish.

CHAMPIGNONS AUX ÉPICES

Spiced mushrooms, the recipe of Madame Dijour of Faucon. Serves 4.

1lb/450g button mushrooms
2fl oz/50ml ($\frac{1}{4}$ cup) olive oil
4fl oz/100ml ($\frac{1}{2}$ cup) water
4fl oz/100ml ($\frac{1}{2}$ cup) white wine
1 tsp/5ml ground cummin
1 tsp/5ml coriander seeds
4 large cloves garlic, unpeeled and crushed
juice 1 lemon
salt to taste
plenty of black pepper

Simmer all ingredients together, covered for 10–15 minutes. Test for softness, and taste. Continue to cook, but quite fast with lid off, until juice and mushrooms are dark golden but not burning.

TOTÈNES FARCIES AUX HERBES VERTES
ET AUX PIGNONS

*Baby squid stuffed with green herbs and pine kernels in a
tomato and mayonnaise sauce. If you hesitate to cook squid,
try this dish and be converted. Recipe of Pierre and Jany
Gleize of La Bonne Etape, Château-Arnoux. Serves 6.*

3 squid, 10 inches/25cm long
2 tbs/30ml olive oil
1 anchovy fillet, rinsed and cut up
9oz/250g spinach, parsley and Swiss chard, chopped
(or half spinach, half parsley)
2 knobs butter
2oz/50g ($\frac{1}{4}$ cup) diced bacon
1 handful pine kernels
1 tbs/15ml fennel seeds
1 egg, beaten
1 handful breadcrumbs
salt and pepper, to taste
14fl oz/350ml (1$\frac{3}{4}$ cups) tomato sauce (see page 63)

FOR THE MAYONNAISE

2 eggs yolks
1 tsp/5ml Dijon mustard, made up
about 4fl oz/100ml ($\frac{1}{2}$ cup) olive oil

Separate the pockets from the tentacles of the squid and clean.
Reserve pockets to be stuffed. Cut tentacles into dice, and sauté in
1 tbs/15ml olive oil. Soften anchovy in the oil.

Cook chopped herbs and greens gently in butter and reserve.
Frizzle bacon dice until fat runs. Drain bacon. Meanwhile grill (broil)
the pine kernels until light golden.

Mix all the above ingredients together (except squid pockets) with
fennel seeds, beaten egg and breadcrumbs. Season according to taste.
Stuff each squid pocket with a small amount of mixture, as they
shrink in cooking. Sew up pockets or hold together with cocktail
sticks. Season. Colour lightly in olive oil and butter, then transfer to
oven dish, and surround with tomato sauce. Leave in gentle oven,
300°F/150°C/Gas Mark 2, until squid is cooked.

Meanwhile, make a mayonnaise with 2 egg yolks, mustard and
olive oil, taking care to beat the oil in gradually. When cool, strain the
sauce from the cooked *Totènes*, and mix with mayonnaise. Slice
Totènes and place in sauce on individual plates.

SARDINES CRUES

*Monsieur Mouret of the St-Hubert, Entrechaux, serves his
marinaded sardines with red and blackcurrant relish made
at least two weeks in advance. Madame Peyraud of
Domaine Tempier serves hers in olive oil with chopped
chives, tomato (skinned and seeded) in small cubes,
with salt and pepper.*

RELISH

½lb/225g red and/or blackcurrants
6fl oz/150ml (¾ cup) red wine vinegar
2fl oz/50ml (¼ cup) white wine

For each person

3 or 4 very fresh sardines, boned
juice of ½ lemon

To make the relish, steep the currants for at least 15 days in the
vinegar and wine. It will keep for about two months, just the length of
the best season for sardines.

Descale the sardines thoroughly by passing between thumb and
fingers, from tail to head and back again. Scales will drop off easily.
Rinse well in cold water. Bone and open out flat. Squeeze lemon juice
over sardines 10 minutes before eating.

Decorate with lemon slices and the relish. Serve with wholemeal
(whole-wheat) bread.

Café des Nattes, Avignon

SALADE MECHOUÏA

OK but sweet,

Red and green pepper salad with onion-and-raisin relish. Recipe of Algerian cook, Mimi, at Café des Nattes, Avignon. Serves 6.

5 or 6 firm red and green peppers
a few black (ripe) olives
2 tbs/30ml olive oil
a little vinegar
salt
black pepper

RELISH

1lb/450g baby onions (fresh or frozen)
8fl oz/200ml (1 cup) water
2fl oz/50ml ($\frac{1}{4}$ cup) wine vinegar
3 tbs/45ml olive oil
2oz/50g ($\frac{1}{4}$ cup) sugar
3 tbs/45ml tomato purée (paste)
3oz/75g ($\frac{1}{2}$ cup) raisins
bouquet garni
salt, pepper

Open out the peppers, de-seed, and flatten on a baking tray (sheet), skin side up. Grill (broil) at a high temperature until skins are black. Pack them

into a plastic bag and close, excluding all air. Leave for $\frac{1}{2}$ hour, then the blackened skins will easily detach from the flesh. Cut in pieces, add the olives, and serve with olive oil and a touch of vinegar, with seasoning to taste. Makes an excellent starter just like that, but is even better with the onion-and-raisin relish.

To make the relish, simmer all ingredients uncovered for about 45 minutes, until onions are tender and almost no liquid left. Take out bouquet garni, and serve at room temperature.

OMELETTE AUX TRUFFES

*Don't try to feed the multitude or your truffle
omelette will be no miracle!*

For each person

2 eggs
1 tsp water
salt, pepper
1 truffle
knob butter

Mix beaten eggs with a little water, salt and
pepper. Clean truffle and slice not too thinly; add
to mixture. If possible leave covered in fridge
overnight.

Melt a small knob of butter in an omelette pan.
When melted and very hot (but not burned), turn
down heat a little and pour in mixture. When
omelette is nearly cooked, fold over, leaving it a
little liquid, and serve.

ANCHOÏADE

*An anchovy relish to accompany raw vegetables.
Already mentioned in The Magic Hour, it also
makes a classic Provençal starter. Serves 4.*

7 or 8 salted anchovy fillets
1 large clove garlic
1 tsp/5ml olive oil
1 tsp/5ml wine vinegar
large sprig thyme

Rinse the anchovy fillets under the tap and then
leave in water for $\frac{1}{2}$ hour to soak. Pound the garlic
in a mortar, then add the carefully drained
anchovies and pound well with the garlic. Add a
trail of olive oil, the same of wine vinegar, and the
leaves of thyme.

Spread the mixture on French bread and grill
(broil) till golden, preferably in front of an open
fire. The smell of this operation tantalizes your
guests into uncontrollable drooling.

Omelette aux truffes

AÏGO-BOULIDO

Translated literally as 'boiled water', this tonic garlic soup is a winter favourite (mentioned in my opening chapter) of two chefs, Nadine Latour and Marie-Anne Founès. Reputed to revive one after a binge, influenza or an operation.

For each person

6fl oz/150ml (¾ cup) lightly salted water
3 or 4 cloves garlic
1 tsp/5ml olive oil
1 bay leaf
pinch dried sage
pinch dried thyme
1 egg
1 slice toast (optional)
1oz/25g (⅓ cup) grated Parmesan or Gruyère cheese (optional)

Crush the cloves of garlic in their skins and put into salted water with the olive oil. Boil for 10 minutes. Add the herbs. Cover and leave for 10 minutes. Take out garlic and herbs. Beat an egg into each soup bowl and pour hot liquid over it, beating it all the time. If you like, submerge a slice of toast, covered with grated cheese in each bowl of soup.

PÂTES AU PISTOU

Pestou, spelt as in Italian, is the Provençal for small-leaved basil. It becomes pistou on French menus, as in this recipe for noodles with pistou sauce. Serves 4 as a starter.

SAUCE
6 big cloves garlic, peeled
1 large fistful small-leaved basil
2oz/50g (⅔ cup) grated Parmesan cheese
handful pine kernels
2 tomatoes, skinned, seeded and crushed (optional)
3 tbs/45ml olive oil

PASTA
12oz/350g noodles
1 tbs/15ml olive oil
1oz/25g (⅓ cup) grated Parmesan cheese (optional)

For the sauce, pound garlic and basil to a paste with a pestle and mortar. Add cheese, pine kernels and tomatoes (if used), and pound again. Stirring continuously with pestle, add olive oil in a thin stream until you have a thick, pungent green cream.

Cook noodles in lots of boiling salted water with the olive oil. Drain and mix with the pistou sauce. Serve hot, with more grated cheese if you like.

Pâtes au pistou

La Ciotat

BOUILLABAISSE AND COMPANY

*Be kind enough, baggage, to tell your mother not
to forget my daily Bouillabaisse, nor my shell fish. That's
my diet! First thing, shell fish. Midday, Bouillabaisse.
Evening, Aïoli. Don't forget, M'amselle Fanny!*
MARCEL PAGNOL, *FANNY*

There is more Marseilles myth and fallacy
surrounding *bouillabaisse* than any other fish
dish on earth. Everyone claims to have had
their Ultimate Experience; one food writer
even found it in London! Cleverly the restaurant
had the essential *rascasse*, but there was no mention of the small rockfish, sold on local quaysides
collectively as *bouillabaisse*, which give the
fish stock its specific northern Mediterranean
flavour.

Marcel telling a fishy tale

Nineteenth-century Provençal cookbook writer J.-B. Reboul instances some forty usable fish including such untranslateable local exotica as *sard*, *murène*, *roucan*, *girelle*, *pageot*, and *galinette*. Certain fish found in northern waters as well as the Mediterranean are included: soft-shell crabs, mussels, bass, John Dory, whiting, weever fish, monkfish, red mullet and gurnard. A minimum of four different fish for a minimum of eight people is a golden rule, so a *Bouillabaisse* is just as possible in Brixton and Brooklyn as on a Marseilles waterfront – although it will never taste quite the same.

As in Marseilles, so in Harrods fish department – it depends on the Catch of the Day. Personally I would rather have a Dover sole in London, Clam Chowder in New York, and leave the *Bouillabaisse* for a treat on the Côte d'Azur, but there are more adventurous cooks than me. And no book on this region, even if you don't feel that adventurous,

would be worth its saltwater without a *Bouillabaisse* experience.

With typical Marseillais exaggeration, there are as many 'best' and 'worst' *Bouillabaisses* as varieties of fish in Reboul. 'Marseilles has had it. Go to Bacon at Cap d'Antibes!' 'Antibes?!!! What about L'Escale at Carry-le-Rouet?' 'Compared to Minguela's?' 'No, no, no – the Calypso!' 'Georges doesn't marinade!' 'Marius poisoned Matilde with his *rascasse*!' 'Charley's strictly for tourists!'

Our own 'Best *Bouillabaisse*' was way off the tourist beat. Indeed off anyone's beat, even a helpful gendarme's. After many wrong turns in a bleak Marseilles suburb, we were told to turn left on the Corniche, go as far as we could, and we would see signs to 'Chez Aldo'. It was the last *calanque*, they told us. Any moment I expected to meet my French connection unloading his boat.

Lurking beneath a massive, rugged hill with strips of grey rock and green *maquis*, the louche fishing port of Montredon basked in steamy sun-

Marseilles calanque

Bringing in the morning catch- La Ciotat

shine. Shack-like buildings, the chimney of a small factory, a bright pink bar where men in dark glasses lounged. Tough, swarthy kids were playing near beat-up cars. And through the heat haze of the oil-calm sea, the city of Marseilles shimmered, with the occasional gunlike flash as sunlight struck a passing car on the Corniche.

'Chez Aldo', when we found it, appeared to be a pizzeria, and we had not exactly come all this way for pizza. But we were soon reassured by the maritime background of the much-travelled owner, Max Veron. Born a few kilometres away at Pointe Rouge, Max went to sea at seventeen, washed dishes, cooked, and waited on table. After managing another restaurant, he bought this modest pizzeria which also specialized in the freshest of fish. Life had a strong tang around 'Chez Aldo'. Posters of action movies (*Mad Max, Rocky III, Rambo II*) alternated with dried turtles, giant crabs, lobsters and a hungry-looking shark

on the wall. Why not 'Chez Max', I asked? Max said he had kept the original name as a tribute to the former owner Aldo, a great character, very popular in the neighbourhood, with a *Bouillabaisse* it was hard to beat.

'And I'm keeping up the tradition,' Max said, giving a wave through the big windows overlooking the port. He liked the restaurant's position: he could make signals to his fishermen, Marcel and Francis, as their boats came in.

Selon l'arrivage on the menu is the sign of a fish restaurant's seriousness. 'Like hunting,' Max said, 'you never know what'll be in the bag.' Marcel, nut brown, had just landed his catch of the day and was selling it beneath an orange parasol on the quayside. He handed Max a blue plastic bag filled with fish. Max didn't even look inside. 'I trust the boys. They know what I like. If it's bad weather and they can't put out, my clients get pizza!'

Marcel and Francis are artisanal fisherman, perfectionists. In fact *Bouillabaisse* began as a fisherman's soup, cooked out on the beach in a

La Ciotat harbour

huge cauldron on a driftwood fire, using the fish not good enough to sell. Nowadays even comparatively simple fresh fish is a luxury only three per cent of the Marseillais can afford. 'Let's exaggerate – say five per cent!' said Marcel. 'Even so, I make a good living, because there's no middle man ripping me off like those poor Drôme lamb-farmers. But it's hard work, very tough. I never go more than forty-five minutes away, but then I have to encircle the rocks with a net eighty metres long, which can only be done in a small boat. These rocks are rich in molluscs and certain herbs and plankton which the rockfish feed on and give the *Bouillabaisse* its special taste.'

It is not by chance that Max is supplied by two fishermen: Marcel and Francis each have their own fishing-ground. Marcel's is sheltered from the east wind, Francis's from the mistral, so it is rarely such bad weather that Max goes without fish.

He had prepared our *Bouillabaisse* well in advance, putting the main fish to marinade – the only correct traditional procedure, according to him. Ordering the day before was another must. 'If you come in off the street for a *Bouillabaisse*, how can it be marinaded for the minimum two hours? Some of those tourist dumps are a con.' And with disarming lack of modesty he continued: 'The owners of six top Marseilles restaurants came here, and all voted mine the best *Bouillabaisse*. I've never been in a good food guide

– and I never will! I don't need Monsieur Gault or Millau telling me how to cook.'

The fish were *rascasse*, *roucan*, red mullet, red gurnard, John Dory, weever fish and conger eel. And Max's marinade consisted of tomatoes, onions, peppers, garlic, olive oil, saffron, fennel. 'With the fish impregnated with these flavours, the actual cooking is comparatively simple,' he explained. 'You make a fish stock, using similar ingredients to the marinade, plus potatoes and little rockfish. Plunge the marinaded fish into boiling fish stock, and the cold fish stops it boiling. When it boils up again, lower the flame. That's where the name comes from: *bouillir* (boil) and *baisser* (lower). But the cooking must be fast. After ten minutes, take out everything but the potatoes, which help thicken the soup.'

Bouillabaisse is a two-course dish – soup followed by fish and potatoes. But before we began, the little white wine of Cassis was poured, its traditional accompaniment. Then we put three rounds each of toast in our soup plates, having rubbed them vigorously with garlic (Max always has fifty kilos in store), and given each of them a daub of *rouille*, that spicy red-chilli and garlic sauce, and grated Gruyère; followed by ladlefuls of pungent soup, with its perfectly blended flavours.

The only problem: to leave room for the second course. The fish was carried in with due ceremony, and displayed on its long, silver plate by two proud young waiters. Max smiled like a wily old cat, pleased at our pleasure. 'The fish should always be shown whole,' he said. 'Proof of its freshness, it didn't fall to bits in the cooking.'

With loving care, the waiters filleted the fish, served a portion to each of us, plus potatoes moistened with a little soup. Aromaquatic is all I can describe it as, a taste experience of sun, sea and herbs as I had only had once before. Quite the Best Bouillabaisse in Marseilles. Naturally.

My first Best Bouillabaisse had been at the long-ago St-Tropez of *yé yé* and Brigitte Bardot. I used to play *pétanque* in Place des Lices with a fisherman, a mason, and a garage mechanic who each claimed to make the best *Bouillabaisse*. They combined efforts and the result, made at our temporary home at nearby Grimaud, hooked me on it for life. There was also *Bourride*, that less complicated but equally rich fish soup, a speciality of Leï Mouscardins, a rather stuffy but classic butter-and-cream restaurant overlooking the port, in the days when tryglycerides were a mere word in a medical dictionary and polenta was strictly for tribesmen. *Aïoli*, the garlic mayonnaise beloved of Tropéziens, accompanied it.

You will find fish suitable for *Bourride* at home, as described in the recipe at the end of the chapter. Fish not exclusively Mediterranean but used nowadays in Provençal dishes (sardines, salmon, skate, sole, trout, bream, salt cod, clams, tuna, inkfish, squid, octopus) are in evidence, albeit somewhat haphazardly, at the smallest markets of Provence, up to a hundred miles from the coast. Once out of the refrigerated trucks, there are heat

problems; many fish shops close down altogether in high summer. Friday, when fish is still a must for practising Roman Catholics, is the best day to buy fresh. We avoid Monday. Though we are never quite pushed to the extremes of poor Smollett, suffering the rigours of eighteenth-century Provence:

As I was not disposed to eat stinking fish, with ragouts of eggs and onions, I insisted upon a leg of mutton, and a brace of fine partridges, which I found in the larder.

Nowadays, thanks to the inventiveness of Provençal chefs, fish dishes are often the most intriguing on the menu, as I hope the recipes at the end of this chapter show. But a lot of fishy chichi goes on. As Pierre Gleize says: 'Who needs lobster in a *Bouillabaisse*? It's as bad as putting champagne in a Kir, just so you can call it Royal.' The Gleizes work wonders with the humble cod. Take their *Morue fraiche à la Dénostin*. First, a

translation of this strange word *Dénostin*: it is a jokey Provençal concoction meaning 'of our time' (*de nos temps*). The fresh cod is lightly fried in *tapénade*, and served with a sauce containing tomato, lemon, ground almonds, saffron and a few shavings of bitter chocolate. Even the testy Smollett could not have resisted that.

One of L'Oustau de Baumanière's most popular dishes is Red Mullet Fillets with a Basil Sauce. And Michel Bosc did specially for us Rascasse Fillets wrapped in Cabbage Leaves with Pastis.

Nadine Latour's delicious *Feuilleté* of Trout Fillets and Spinach is an impressive dish to serve. Also a Fish Terrine with Dill Sauce. Then, when we're feeling really lazy, there's nothing like barbecuing a few fresh sardines with sprigs of savory from the garden.

The harbour fish shop

BOURRIDE

Like Bouillabaisse, this fish soup from Sète is a meal in itself.
But unlike Bouillabaisse, it can be made with any firm white fish,
such as seabass, sea-bream, whiting, grey mullet or turbot.
The Sètois make it with lotte de mer (monkfish).
Served with Aïoli essentially, and Rouille optionally. Serves 6.

2lb/900g firm white fish
2 pints/1 litre (4½ cups) water
4fl oz/100ml (½ cup) white wine
1 onion, chopped
slice of lemon
curl of orange peel
½tsp/2.5ml salt
pepper
1 bay leaf
bunch of fennel and thyme
3 egg yolks
3 tbs/30ml cream
toasted French bread, to serve
2 cloves garlic

Interestg.
Good.

Clean fish and cut into thick slices. Put water into a large pan and add wine, onion, lemon, orange peel, seasoning and herbs. Bring to boil, put in fish and simmer 12–15 minutes or until just cooked. Lift fish on to deep serving dish and keep warm.

Make double quantity of the Aïoli recipe below. Divide it into two, keeping half to serve with the bourride. To the other half of the Aïoli, add the egg yolks and cream, stirring well. Then pour little by little into the warm fish stock, still stirring. Over very gentle heat, with wooden spoon, continue to stir until sauce coats spoon, and soup is smooth and creamy. It must not boil.

First serve this soup with rounds of toasted French bread, rubbed with garlic and topped with Rouille. Then serve the fish with lots of boiled potatoes, some more soup poured over, and a dollop of the remaining Aïoli.

Bourride, Restaurant Peron

AÏOLI

good but heavy.

Traditionally served with Bourride, this garlic mayonnaise is also served with crudités (raw vegetables), and in the feast of Le Grand Aïoli, described in the first chapter. Serves 3.

2 cloves garlic, peeled
1 egg yolk
¼ pint/150ml (⅔ cup) best quality olive oil
warm water
lemon juice
salt and pepper

Egg and oil must be at room temperature.
Pound garlic to a paste with pestle and mortar (about 5 minutes). Stir in egg yolk thoroughly, then start to add oil little by little. When the mixture thickens, add a little water and lemon juice, then more oil. Repeat this operation until you have enough Aïoli. Season with salt and pepper.
If Aïoli separates in the making, put it in another bowl, clean the mortar, put another egg yolk in with a few drops of lemon juice and water. Little by little, pour in the aïoli, stirring all the time. It will reconstitute itself.
This mayonnaise can be fairly liquid or stiff enough to stand up a pestle. Both are equally good – it's the taste that counts.

ROUILLE

good.

A spicy-hot reddish condiment, also served with Bouillabaise, poached white fish, cod, squid, and boiled potatoes.

3 cloves garlic
½ red chilli (chilli pepper)
chunk stale white bread
3 tbs/45ml olive oil

Soak red pepper overnight if dried. Remove seeds and wash hands. Soak the bread in water and squeeze dry. With pestle and mortar, pound garlic and red pepper to a paste. Add bread and pound again. Add oil until you have a very thick, red cream.
Serve with poached white fish, stirring a little fish stock into your rouille.

FEUILLETÉ DE TRUITE AUX ÉPINARDS

*Trout and spinach in flaky pastry. Recipe from Madame
Latour, of Domaine de la Cabasse, Séguret, whose version
has more layers. This one is simpler for the home cook and is
served with a coulis de tomate (tomato sauce). Serves 6–8.*

1½lb/700g (3 cups) flaky pastry (can be frozen)
2lbs/1kg spinach (if frozen, use leaf-spinach, not chopped)
3 shallots, chopped
1oz/25g (2tbs) butter
4 pink trout, skinned and filleted
salt and pepper to taste

COULIS DE TOMATE

2 onions, chopped
2 tbs/30ml olive oil
2lb/1kg tomatoes, skinned, seeded and chopped
(or 1 large can of tomatoes)
4 cloves garlic, crushed
1tsp/5ml sugar
bouquet garni, especially basil
salt and pepper, to taste

Take half the pastry and roll it out to about ⅛ inch/3mm thick to make a rectangle about 12×15 inches/30×37cm, or a size that fits your oven. Oil a baking sheet, lay the pastry on it and prick well all over with a fork. Bake in a pre-heated oven, 400°F/200°C/Gas Mark 6 for 25–30 minutes, until pastry is just turning golden. Take out and allow to cool. Repeat this operation with the other half of the pastry.

Wash the spinach well, boil for 5 minutes in a little salted water, then drain thoroughly. (If frozen, thaw out the spinach and drain.) Meanwhile fry the shallots gently in the butter until soft.

Beat the fillets carefully to an even thickness.

Put one pastry layer on the oiled baking sheet, spread out the spinach on it, then lay the trout fillets on top of the spinach. Sprinkle with the chopped shallots and salt and pepper. Lay the second pastry on top, and return the baking sheet to the oven, now at 350°F/180°C/Gas Mark 4, for 20 minutes, or until the pastry is golden brown and the fish is cooked.

Allow to cool a little before cutting for serving, or the pastry will break.

To make the tomato sauce, soften the onion in the oil. Add all the other ingredients and simmer for about 45 minutes, squashing the tomatoes with a wooden spoon. Blend or process very briefly to a purée, or the rich red colour will go paler.

RASCASSE AU CHOU

*Rascasse fillets wrapped in cabbage leaves, a recipe of Monsieur Bosc,
of Bistrot à Michel, Cabrières-d'Avignon. The court bouillon
can be home made (see Terrine de Poissons) or use a cube. Serves 5–6.*

3 shallots, chopped small
1 leek, diced
3 carrots, diced
3½oz/100g (⅓ cup) butter
8fl oz/200ml (1 cup) white wine
5 or 6 large dark green leaves savoy cabbage
1 big rascasse, filleted (or 2 small ones)
½ pint/300ml (1¼ cups) court bouillon
⅓oz/10g (1 tbs) thinly sliced truffle
6 basil leaves, chopped
pepper and salt, to taste
⅓ pint/200ml (¾ cup) thin (pouring) cream
a little pastis

To decorate

baby tomatoes
small sprigs parsley
2tsp/10ml thyme

Make a *brunoise* by gently frying the chopped shallots, leek and carrots in butter till almost soft. Add white wine and continue cooking to reduce a little.

Meanwhile, cut out the thick centre stem of cabbage leaves and boil green parts for 5 minutes in salted water. Rinse well in cold water and dry. If fillets of fish are very thick, score with a knife. Cut into serving portions.

Add the court bouillon to the *brunoise*, bringing to the boil. Put in fish fillets and cook, covered, over medium heat for no more than 5 minutes. Take out fillets with fish slice and wrap each one in cabbage. Put these bundles carefully back into the *brunoise* pan over a gentle heat, just to take the flavour. Then take them out and keep warm in serving dish.

Make a sauce of the fish stock mixture by adding finely sliced truffle, basil leaves, pepper and salt (careful with this), and cream. Cook gently till sauce coats the back of the spoon. Off the heat add a dash of pastis, put back on heat, stir briefly, then pour sauce round fish fillets. Decorate with tomato and tiny sprigs of parsley and thyme.

TERRINE DE POISSONS

Our recipe for fish terrine with dill sauce. For the white fish, whiting, angler-fish, sea-bass, brill, or John Dory are best. The court bouillon can be made by boiling up fish heads and bones and reserving liquid. Serves 6–8.

1¾lb/800g firm white fish
2¼lb/1kg rock salmon
12oz/350g pink trout
salt and pepper
2 pints/1.2 litres (5 cups) court bouillon
4fl oz/100ml (½ cup) dry white wine
2 cloves garlic
bouquet garni
2 tsp/10ml gelatine powder

SAUCE

big bunch fresh dill
¾ pint/450ml (2 cups) thin (pouring) cream
1 tbs/15ml lemon juice
salt and pepper to taste

Put fish in seasoned court bouillon with white wine, garlic and bouquet garni. Bring slowly to boil, then take off heat. The fish should be cooked. Reserve bouillon. Skin and bone fish, keeping aside some big pink and white pieces. Process or blend rest of fish with a little of the bouillon to make a thick creamy mixture.

Mix gelatine with ½ pint/300ml (1¼ cups) warm court bouillon. Coat large, deep tin (pan) or dish with gelatine, let set, then fill with alternate layers of creamed fish and fish pieces, ending with a thin layer of gelatine. Put in freezer to set. Transfer to fridge 3 hours before turning out. Keep in fridge until serving time. A slice of terrine is placed on each person's plate after the sauce, not before.

To make the sauce, chop the dill (the more the better) and stir into cream. Add lemon juice, salt and pepper to taste.

FILETS DE ROUGET AU BASILIC

Red mullet fillets with basil sauce. Prepare sauce two days in advance. Recipe of Monsieur Charial and Monsieur Thuilier of L'Oustau de Baumanière, Les Baux. Serves 4.

1 tomato
1 bunch basil
scant ½ pint/275ml (1 cup) best olive oil
¼ clove garlic
½ shallot, finely chopped
½ tsp/2.5ml sherry vinegar (*vinaigre de xérès*)
salt and pepper to taste
2 bay leaves
4 red mullets (about 7½oz/210g each) filleted

To decorate

4 olives
1tbs/15ml chopped basil
4 small tomatoes

Peel, seed and chop tomato. Chop basil leaves finely. Add to olive oil, with crushed garlic, shallot, bay leaves, sherry vinegar, salt and pepper. Leave 1–2 days to macerate and enrich flavour.

Season the red mullet fillets and steam for about 3 minutes. Remove bay leaves from sauce mixture. To serve, put a spoonful of sauce on each plate, arrange the fillets on top. Decorate each plate with an olive, chopped basil, and tiny tomatoes.

Rouget au basilic

MONSIEUR BOEUF'S
LAMB

*The men of High Provence speak little; the game
they play is entirely within themselves. . . .*
JEAN GIONO, *RONDEUR DES JOURS*

Had we got the time of our appointment wrong? Ducks were on the pond, chickens under the lime trees, rabbits in hutches, bees in the lavender, and a lame ewe in the sheepfold. But not a human being in sight. Then Lucienne Boeuf appeared at the front door, a look of only faint surprise on her lived-in, humorous face. It had happened before, with other visitors to the farm. We were not expected till an hour later, because her sheep-farmer husband, Julien Boeuf, doesn't believe in

The Boeufs' farm, Rémuzat

The Drôme hills

Summer Time and keeps his grandfather clock an hour behind the rest of France.

'He likes the light mornings,' Madame Boeuf explained. 'But he also keeps getting the time wrong for the television news, which he does not like at all.' The huge television was the only modern furnishing of the spare, spotless living-room: it sat on a treadle sewing-machine table; there were dried thistles, a crucifix, brass candlesticks, a china fox, a niche for pastis and mint syrup; the tiled floor was the playground of five tiny shaggy sheepdogs and a gang of cats. Then Chantal, the Boeufs' grand-daughter, their only permanent help on the farm, brought in a convivial cock which joined the conversation with intermittent crowings.

I commented on the delicious smell wafting from the kitchen. '*Ragoût de mouton*' said Madame Boeuf. 'There's nothing like it – except perhaps lamb chops grilled on a wood fire.'

As long, of course, as it was Monsieur Boeuf's lamb. 'I've nothing against you British,' he had confided on my last visit, 'except Madame Thatcher. She looks after her own farmers too well, that one, and the Common Market can go to hell!' I had hoped to hear his current views on *la Dame de Fer*, but now, two years later, Monsieur Boeuf had grown deaf, hated his hearing-aid, and was becoming something of a recluse.

Speaking for her husband, Madame Boeuf made mountain lamb-raising sound deceptively easy: 'Our 220 lambs are up there on the plateau, eating nothing but grass and herbs. Born in March, sold before the end of the year, they're brought up naturally, wild in the mountains. And that gives them a specially good taste.' But that taste was hard come by.

Born in 1909 at Nyons, Julien merged his land with Lucienne's, and in 1933 they borrowed money to develop their joint farm. A brave move in those days. There was no road to this lonely

Lucienne Boeuf, Chantal and cockerel

Monsieur Boeuf

hillside, high above Rémuzat; it was five kilometres on horseback down to the valley.

Then came the war. Julien was taken prisoner in the first year, and, refusing to work for the Nazis, found himself in the notorious death camp of Rawa Ruska.

During the Occupation, the farm was a hideaway for Resistance fighters, and eventually the Germans burned it. But the Boeufs had a windfall. Wrongly informed that her husband was dead, Lucienne picked up her war widow's pension for eighteen months – and this came in very handy for rebuilding the ruin.

Julien, a big man with fine twirly moustaches, weighed a mere forty kilos when he returned. But his energy was boundless. Eminently practical, he fixed up the new farm with two electricity supplies; and when I last saw him, aged seventy-

eight, was still hard at work, building a new trailer.

Award plaques came thick and fast over the sheepfold. Holder of the Légion d'Honneur for services to French agriculture, Julien campaigned tirelessly for the quality which makes the lamb of the Pré-Alpes du Sud so special – and the best meat of Provence. And he still had time for his hobbies: beekeeping, carving shepherd's crooks (he made one for the Bishop of the Drôme) and writing his memoirs.

But recently a change had come over Julien Boeuf. 'My husband has aged badly,' Madame Boeuf confided. Without rancour, even with a certain wry humour, she continued: 'I own another property – a twenty-hectare vineyard at Vinsobres, totally neglected. It would have been much easier work for us, this late in life. But no – you see, that's mine. And he can only farm what's his.'

As we watched the old man moving about quietly in the pine trees among his beehives, helmeted as though to escape recognition, the

Sheepfold with awards

melancholy of the Boeuf farm struck me. As if echoing my thoughts, Madame Boeuf spoke with touching frankness: 'Who'll take over from him? We've no son – neither of our daughters wanted to farm. So there's just Chantal. What kind of life is it for a modern girl? She'll want holidays. I never even *thought* of holidays.' Madame Boeuf sighed. 'I'll be eighty next year. And, you know, farming's a dying art – in this old way. Now it's the turn of the big, industrialized farms on the plain.'

A sense of impending tragedy lay behind the shady lime trees, tinkling streams, and natural splendour of these Drôme sheep hills.

Up another winding road, tortuous hairpin bends making the car screech for mercy and my head spin with vertigo, we visited farmers worse off than the Boeufs, though one would never know it from their hospitality and lack of complaint.

With one pig, a little hay and lavender, Monsieur and Madame Léon Laget live on their small-holding in Breughel-esque circumstances. 'Twenty years ago we sold a live animal for ten francs a kilo,' Madame Laget told us. 'Nowadays it's only fourteen francs – nowhere near keeping up with inflation.' Perhaps her daughter, who had upped and away and married a Paris businessman, sent them money; perhaps not. 'Often the young don't marry here because they don't meet anyone. The sons and daughters who stay are like prisoners of the farm.'

Their neighbour is just such a son. A fine, cheerful man of indeterminate age with a mouthful of gold teeth, he looks after a few straggly vines and his senile eighty-two-year-old mother, who no longer knows who he is. This man, though he could have done with the money, recently refused to sell land to a French friend of ours living a mere thirty kilometres away, because even coming from so near he counted as a 'foreigner'.

For the young it is a choice of evils: stay and suffer in silence, or desert a heritage. Jean Giono was the prophet of this flight from the land, the dying of a certain life which, however tough, had its own quality. A quality reflected in its produce. Who, lunching in splendour on the terrace of L'Oustau de Baumanière, would make any connection between the succulent *Gigot d'agneau en croûte* on their plate and the Julien Boeufs of this world? Yet each depends on the other.

There may still be a future for past ways in a revival of interest in the recipes of *les anciens*. Meat consumption in France has doubled in the last twenty-five years; and the comparitively wealthy farmers of the Rhône Valley are no exception. But Bernard Ely, retired doctor of preventative medicine, has organized a study group of their wives into a move away from a diet of steaks and joints of pork to the lighter, healthier meat-eating habits of their more frugal forbears. Specifically, Docteur Ely instanced the wonderful Provençal peasant soups of meat and vegetables which, like *Bouillabaisse*, could be two-course meals.

In his cool, high-ceilinged Avignon apartment, Docteur Ely introduced us to *La bajana*. A small piece of ham was cooking slowly with vegetables in a *bouillon*, chick-peas in another pan. First, you ate the soup, poured over bread rubbed with garlic; after that, you had the ham, chick-peas, and vegetables.

Then there is *Soupe d'épeautre*, made with spelt, a rare kind of mountain wheat rather like barley; and equally delicious, *La rato rato*. The first is supposed to contain a ham bone; we make both with a particularly good local pork-rind sausage – *saucisse de couenne*.

This sausage comes from our excellent butcher, Georges Gugliemenetti of Tulette. Monsieur Georges is a Burgundian who did his apprentice-ship at nearby Camaret; after a stint as butcher in the smart seventeenth *arrondissement* of Paris, he and Madame Georges, a chic, fine-looking Parisienne, came south to the sun of this little market town.

Up at six, and closing shop at seven in the evening, Monsieur Georges still finds time to make his own *pâté de campagne*, calf's head salad, stuffed veal, stuffed tomatoes, epigrams of lamb, rolled-and-boned legs of turkey, and the regional specialities *caillettes* and *pieds et paquets*. When we asked him for the recipe for *caillettes* – pork fag-gots, highly seasoned and herbed, Monsieur Georges hesitated a moment, glanced at Madame Georges for her approval, then whispered as though giving away part of a state secret: 'One-third minced pork, one-third pig's liver, one-third spinach. The rest I must leave to you.' We tried, and now we buy *caillettes* from him.

Courage failed us completely with *pieds et paquets*, a complicated but delicious Marseillais speciality consisting of a lamb's foot, with two stuffed lamb's tripe 'packets', tied with thin edible 'strings' also made of lamb's tripes. Rest assured that, in the expert hands of a butcher like Monsieur Georges, 'Feet and Packets' should not be missed, despite its name, but certainly not attempted for Sunday lunch in Wiltshire. Better to stick to our own favourite *Gigot provençale* – a leg of lamb spiked with garlic, surrounded by onions, tomatoes, peppers and sprigs of rosemary,

The Lagets' farm

Madame Laget chasing her pig

moistened with half a tumbler each of olive oil and water. We first tasted this at Bargemon where, along with other families' Sunday joints, it was baked in the baker's oven. It started cooking covered with tin-foil, which was taken off thirty minutes before we went to fetch it, all brown and succulent. The vegetables and cooking juices made an unforgettable sauce.

Monsieur Georges also provides impeccable meat for a winter Stuffed Cabbage and a summer Veal Casserole with Green Olives and Sage; and for our year-round *daubes*, those traditional casseroles made with beef or lamb, for which every family has a different recipe. Beef cattle are not to be seen in the sun-dried fields of Provence, and beef *daube* is thought to have originated when no one knew what to do with the tough beef of bulls after a Camargue bullfight. Cooking in red wine was the best way to tenderize it.

The bourgeoisie, no doubt, required finer imported beef cuts for such dishes as *Boeuf à la mode du Cardinal Maury*. In 1801 Cardinal Maury of Valréas sent his own recipe to his nephew Louis, a canon at Rome, clearly about to entertain some Very Important Clerics. He gave excellent advice about the cooking of *daubes* in general: 'One should barely hear the liquid laughing. Put the pot on the cinders, where there is very little heat. If the pot boils too quickly, the stew is ruined.' Failing cinders, we do ours in the lowest oven heat possible.

Chez Georges, Tulette

Butcher's shop at night, Ménerbes

BOEUF EN DAUBE PROVENÇALE

This marinated beef casserole is a classic party recipe – a beginner's joy. Start the day before and make more than you need; it's always better the second day and even better the third. Serves 8–10.

4½lb/2kg best stewing beef
7oz/200g (1 cup) diced bacon
2 big onions
3–4 carrots
bouquet garni
bay leaf
2 cloves
nutmeg
3 or 4 juniper berries, crushed
salt and pepper to taste
1 bottle red table wine
4fl oz/100ml (½ cup) vinegar
3–5 cloves garlic
curl of orange peel
about ¾ pint/450ml (2 cups) water

Cut meat in decent-sized cubes each weighing about 3½oz/100g. Marinade with 1 roughly chopped onion, sliced carrots, bouquet garni, bay-leaf, cloves, nutmeg, juniper berries, salt, pepper, red wine and vinegar. Best left covered overnight in fridge.

Next day, in a large frying pan (skillet) with a very little oil, lightly cook cut-up pieces of bacon and 1 onion cut in rounds, till soft. Add the pieces of meat, dried of the marinade juice with a paper towel. Allow to brown. Transfer bacon, onion and meat to heavy iron casserole. Add marinade with all its ingredients, then crushed garlic and orange peel. Add hot water just to cover and bring to boil.

Hermetically seal the casserole with foil. Cook 4–5 hours in a very slow oven, 300°F/150°C/Gas Mark 2. It's ready when you can cut the meat with a spoon. Serve with fresh noodles, over which you have put a ladleful of the meat sauce.

Disappointing results. Meat fork tender but wishy washy. Meat sauce very greasy and liquid. Try to make it a day ahead to decrease the juices and reduce them. A roux did not help. Slightly acid although. I did not add the vinegar. Maybe 300° is too much for cast iron pots.

CHOU FARCI

Our version of Reboul's classic recipe for stuffed cabbage.
Serves 6.

savoy cabbage, weighing about 2lb/900g
7oz/200g (1 cup) lean diced bacon
2 onions
2 slices stale bread
$\frac{1}{2}$ pint/300ml (1$\frac{1}{4}$ cups) milk
5oz/150g ($\frac{2}{3}$ cup) long-grain rice
7oz/200g (1 cup) sausage meat or chopped chicken
1 egg
$\frac{1}{2}$ tsp/2.5ml grated nutmeg
thyme leaves
2 cloves garlic, crushed
salt and pepper
1 pint/600ml (2$\frac{1}{2}$ cups) bouillon or stock cube
3 tbs/45ml tomato purée (paste)
2 carrots
bouquet garni

Throw away damaged coarse leaves and blanch whole cabbage in boiling water for 5 minutes. Drain, refresh with cold water, drain again. Open by pressing back leaves one by one. Cut out heart and chop finely.

For the stuffing, sizzle bacon in a small pan until fat runs. Add 1 chopped onion and soften. Soak bread in milk, then squeeze nearly dry. In a bowl, mix together bacon, onion, chopped cabbage heart, uncooked rice, sausage or chicken meat, bread, beaten egg, nutmeg, thyme and garlic. Season well. Put a good spoonful in middle of cabbage, then in each leaf, remaking the original shape. Tie with kitchen string.

Put in deep oven dish just a little larger than the cabbage. Cover with bouillon mixed with tomato purée (paste), add the chopped carrots, the second onion, sliced, and bouquet garni. Cover and leave for 3 hours or more in a slow oven, 325°F/170°C/Gas Mark 3, until it is slightly brown on top and has absorbed nearly all the liquid, melding all its delicious flavours together.

Used sausage meat. Not too impressed. Skip rice.

RATO RATO

A country soup with spicy, meaty sausages, which is a whole meal in itself. One of those Provençal dishes that needs spoon, knife and fork!

For each person

1 or 2 uncooked sausages, such as Toulouse
little olive oil
½ small onion, chopped
½ tsp/2.5ml tomato purée (paste)
½ pint/300ml (1½ cups) water
pinch of sage
½ clove garlic, crushed
salt and pepper, to taste
1 slice toast
1 tbs/15ml grated cheese

Take 1 or 2 sausages per person, prick them well and fry lightly to release their fat. When golden, take them out and keep warm. Throw away fat. In a little olive oil, sauté onion. Add tomato purée (paste), water, sage, garlic, salt and pepper. Cover and simmer 20–30 minutes.

In each dish, put a slice of toast, the sausage and grated cheese. Pour over the hot soup and serve.

GIGOT D'AGNEAU EN CRÔUTE

Leg of lamb in pastry. Recipe of Monsieur Raymond Thuilier of L'Oustau de Baumanière, Les Baux. The leg of lamb should not weigh more than 2lb/900g. Serves 4–6.

2 lamb's kidneys
2 knobs butter
4fl oz/100ml (½ cup) Madeira
5oz/150g (1¼ cups) button mushrooms, quartered
½ tsp/2.5ml each of thyme, rosemary and tarragon
salt and pepper, to taste
1 leg of lamb, boned
12oz/350g puff pastry
1 egg yolk, beaten

Dice the kidneys and fry in butter. Déglacer with the Madeira, then add mushrooms, herbs and seasoning. Cook on a few minutes. Put mixture in the lamb, filling space left by bone. Close opening with 3 or 4 string stitches.

Rub lamb with a little butter. Put into hot oven 475°F/240°C/Gas Mark 9 for 15 minutes to seize meat and draw out its moisture.

Remove from oven, wrap in thinly rolled puff pastry. Brush with yolk of egg and return to oven for 15–20 minutes to finish cooking if you like your lamb pink. Leave longer if you prefer it well done.

Gigot d'agneau en croûte

VEAU AUX OLIVES VERTES À LA SAUGE *Exc.*

Veal casserole with green olives and sage. Recipe of Madame Campdorasse of Grimaud. Serves 6–8.

2lb/900g best pie veal in large squares
4 strips 3½oz/100g (½ cup) lean diced bacon
12–16 small onions or 2 large ones, quartered
2 cloves garlic, crushed
2 good sprigs sage (or 2 tsp dried sage)
3 tbs/45ml tomato purée (paste)
2 cups 2 wine glasses of white wine
⅓–½ pint/200–300ml (1¼ cups) stock
2 handfuls green olives, stoned (pitted)
7oz/200g (1¾ cups) button mushrooms,
fresh or canned
salt and pepper, to taste

Into a heavy-based casserole pack the veal, bacon, onions, garlic and sage leaves. Mix the tomato purée (paste) with the wine and enough stock to barely cover the meat. Bring to boil and simmer on a very slow heat for 1 hour. Add green olives *small,* and continue cooking, for about ½ hour or until meat is tender. Add mushrooms, season, and stir. After about 10 minutes dish is ready.

Serve with long-grain rice and triangles of fried French bread.

Refrigerate to degrease.
Add 2 Tbsp. flour to make gravy.
Used ossobucco - try
shoulder next time.
Sauce very liquid, try
less stock next time.

RAGÔUT DE MOUTON AUX ARTICHAUTS

For this mutton stew with artichokes choose best end of neck (rack). Recipe of Madame Boeuf of Rémuzat. Serves 6.

3 onions
2½lb/1.25kg lamb, cut into pieces
3 tbs/45ml olive oil
6 potatoes
sprig thyme
salt and pepper, to taste
1 pint/600ml (2½ cups) stock
6 artichoke hearts (optional)

Slice the onions. Heat the olive oil in a heavy-based casserole and brown the meat and onions. Add a little water and cook, covered, on a low heat, for 15 minutes. Peel potatoes and cut into quarters. Place in casserole together with thyme, salt and pepper (no garlic for once!). Cover with stock or water and simmer for 2 hours.

We usually add artichoke hearts 30 minutes before serving. If they are canned, add 5 minutes before serving.

Veau aux olives vertes à la sauge

RED, WHITE, AND PINK

A drunkard never tasted good wine.
PROVENÇAL PROVERB

Playwright Marcel Pagnol, who brought Provençals to the Paris stage as real people not comic yokels as hitherto portrayed, had a Marseilles bar-owner refer to a chilled bottle of Cassis as coming from 'the vineyards of the north pole'. North Pole wine temperatures in southern summers can be a headache – and lead to a bad hangover, too. For the overkill chilling of Midi whites and rosés can disguise their strength – often up to 15°, leaving the unwary weaving about their caravan sites and their caravans about the autoroute.

Knowing the strength of our wine and the weakness of the flesh, the *curé* of Visan told me: 'I

Notre Dame-des-Vignes chapel, Visan

Clos des Papes, a white wine of
Châteauneuf - du - Pape

like my rosé well baptized.' In other words, with a good sprinkling of water. Heresy, some would say, but practical restraint before the thanksgiving service for our summer Fête du Vin. Or, as happened to me this winter, before inauguration as an honorary member of the Confrérie Saint Vincent, the wine brotherhood of Visan, founded in 1475.

This honour is conferred on those 'defending the cause of wine in general and more particularly the wine of Visan'. First, the tasting. I was invited, along with local notables, visiting oenologues and my proposer and former festival Queen, Yvonne Soliva, to the vaulted Saint Vincent cellars of the Cave Coopérative. Here we would choose the best wine for Visan's two most prestigious labels,

Cuvée du Marot (1987) and Saint Vincent (1983). Brothers in Venetian pink capes, wide-brimmed black hats, and red-ribbonned medallions gave it a formal appearance. But any formalities were instantly dispelled by the relaxed, good-humoured welcome for the new honorary member who was all too anxious to uphold Britain's good reputation in the French wine world.

Five was the magic number. Five in each jury, five juries, five bottles of each wine to be tasted. The wine in each came from a different vat and we had to judge the best. My jury swigged, chewed, swilled in the mouth, spat into sawdust – narrowly missing each other – and marked for quality out of ten. 'Plenty of shoulder,' someone commented on a wine's strength; and on its lingering on the palate, 'Plenty of mouth.' But the juries did not agree at all, and the final choice was left to a single jury of experts.

My inauguration then took place at the Confrérie's annual dinner-dance, in the presence of some three hundred Visan *vignerons*, their families, and VIPs in the wine trade. Brothers of the Confrérie entered ceremoniously, bearing their standard. My 'godfather', Monsieur Combe, took the microphone and his speech commended my and Carey's first book, *Views from a French Farmhouse*, for its references to Visan wine. I was presented with a scroll, a red-ribbonned medallion hung round my neck, and our Communist mayor, Pierre Constant, shook my hand warmly,

The procession and Provençal dancing at the Wine Festival, Visan

saying 'Now we're brothers.' Then it was Provençal party time. Long into the night, the five-course feast kept coming, Visan corks kept popping, the band kept rocking and we danced dizzily to pasa dobles, tangoes, and javas played on a genuine *bal musette* accordeon. And when our party left at three in the morning, the meal had only just finished and the band played on.

The winter choice of the Cuvée du Marot, announced during this binge, is important for another wine binge, the August Fête du Vin. Five thousand magnums of this specially good wine of the previous year are interred, to complete their ageing, in the wall of the ruined Marot château. This castle dates from the thirteenth century, when Visan had its first wine press. And the summer wine festival begins with a thanksgiving service.

The lilting tones of a sermon in Provençal made music with the welcome breeze, cooling the August heat. Although I understood only a few sentences, the outdoor service at Our Lady of the Vines, a twelfth-century chapel in a little wood of cypresses and pine trees, aptly combined the Christian and the pagan. After the service Brothers of the Confrérie carried not Saint Vincent, but a vinestock in full leaf, decorated with flowers and bunches of grapes.

We joined the procession to the château. Liveried huntsmen blew calls on their horns. Girls wearing black velvet lace-up bodices, Provençal print skirts, and bonnets, petticoats and stockings

Huntsmen at the Wine Festival, Visan

of dazzling white, danced and sang. Tourists, tongues hanging out for the serious drinking, followed apace.

They had to be patient a little longer. At the château, more singing and dancing, and the vinestock was ceremoniously burned. Incidentally, all this paganism was much too much for 1753's *curé* who banned the ceremony as too bacchanal. Today's *curé* could never get away with that, even if he wanted to.

After Mayor Constant's speech of welcome, poetically interspersed with quotes from Jean Giono in a most untypical mayoral style, Bacchus took over the party. Now we could fall gratefully upon the *buvette* generously dispensing Visan wine, and discover its merits the practical way. Then, as the light changed, it was time for the communal, twilight feast of *Le Grand Aïoli*, already described in the first chapter.

Many such summer wine festivals and tastings happen within a half hour's drive of Visan – Vinsobres, Vacqueyras, Gigondas, Ste-Cécile-des-Vignes, Cairanne, names now regularly seen on labels in New York, London and Paris. Qualities vary from domaine to domaine, and year to year, but we've been blessed with a run of good vintages in the Côtes-du-Rhône (1976, 1978, 1979, 1981, 1983, 1985). Part of the fun is sniffing out good new rosés and whites, more difficult to find than red; a lot depends on good luck or, better still, a good tip-off. Don't stop at the first *Dégus-tation* sign you come to; if it's some great barracks of a winery on a main road, it can lead to a dull tasting. Tasting, by the way, is no obligation to buy. But if you find a *Cave* you like and want to try *all* the wines, you should maybe buy a bottle or two; otherwise, leave smartly the moment you taste the chemical juice. Start with the youngest white, work through to the oldest red, with the rosé in the middle.

Pierre Gleize once intrigued me with a forty-five-year-old white Châteauneuf-du-Pape. It was long past its drinking limit (ten years), but still had faded grandeur, a golden oldie glory which made me long to meet a younger relation. I was told to visit Paul Avril of Clos des Papes.

'We Avrils have been making wine for some three hundred years,' said Monsieur Avril, introducing me to a son also called Paul. 'And all called Paul. We're mainly known for our reds, big wines to put down and keep maybe twenty years or more. White Châteauneuf used to be just for home consumption, but now about thirty of us, out of the 250 winemakers in the Châteuneuf-du-Pape *appellation*, are selling it'. This great *appellation* is second largest in France after St-Emilion.

In the vaulted cellar where Monsieur Avril's father bricked up the best pre-war vintages when the German Occupation began, his son uncorked a 1986 white for us to try. 'Too cold,' he complained. '14°C is about perfect.' We cupped our hands round the bowl of the big tasting glass to reduce the chill a little. Sniffed and tasted. 'A hint of bananas? No?' Well, no. But my palate was not as subtle as that of Paul Avril who could chart his red wine's evolution as it aged – from fruit (gooseberry, raspberry, cherry) via spices (cinnamon and nutmeg) to truffles and nuts. Unlike Châteauneuf red, which has up to thirteen grape varieties in its *cépage*, Clos des Papes white only has five (Roussane, Piqpoul, Bourboulenc, Clairette, and Grenache). Their poetic names matched Monsieur Avril's wine, superbly made, dry and fruity; but I couldn't help wishing we were drinking it with a fish in some delicious sauce or even goat's cheese, food said to be just right to go with it. Monsieur Avril agreed: fine wine is even finer with the right food.

Provence's most picturesque white wine region is on the coast at Cassis. Rare pleasure to stand at sunset among the Ugni, Clairette, and Marsanne vines of Clos Ste-Magdeleine. The vineyard's neat rows run right to the cliff-top. To the east, a mass of reddish brown rock was deepening in the setting sun; to the west, the oily-calm July sea spread beyond a rocky, towering coastline towards Marseilles, the town that loves this *bon p'tit vin* with its fish.

'Cassis is a tiny *appellation*,' said Francis Sack, Polish-born *patron* of Clos Ste-Magdeleine, pointing up to his twenty hectares spreading from the bay in perilous terraces up the side of what looked like a sheer mountain cliff. 'But we're a microclimate here. The mountains create air turbulence and the storms pass us by. We're well aired by sea breezes which kill pests. Ideal conditions for making good wine.'

Although originally from a Parisian furrier's family, Monsieur Sack was now quite *au fait* with a modern *vigneron*'s need to experiment. He had added three per cent of the fashionable Sauvignon grape, which helped give a well-balanced taste. We tasted his Cassis on a twilit terrace overlooking the sea. The wine's finesse and subtlety, he claimed, went best with curry and spicy food – and, of course, *Bouillabaisse*.

A quarter of Monsieur Sack's production was rosé wine. I was always under the misapprehension that rosé was a mixture of white and red wines. Not at all. In fact it is rarely even made from white and black grapes. Normally just with black grapes. These are allowed to ferment a few hours only with their pips and skins, till the juice extracted gives just the right pink. The grape variety, Grenache, which is fifty per cent of a Côtes-du-Rhône red's make-up, also gives a rosé its typically Midi fruitiness.

The grand rosés are Tavel and Lirac. But we enjoy even the grandest with unpretentious, summery things like fresh asparagus, raw vegetables, pâté, barbecued sardines, mountain sausage – things the best picnics are made of.

Sometimes I drive five kilometres down to Le Petit Barbaras, a domaine between Tulette and

Corniche Road from Cassis to La Ciotat

Suze-la-Rousse, for a fill-up *en vrac*. That means that you bring your own container, into which the wine is piped, just like gas into a car's tank. Given the rate of consumption by our summer guests, the fuel merely gets decanted into flasks, cooled in the fridge (not higher than 15°C if possible) and on to the table. A few days in plastic never hurt a Midi rosé.

A very good Bandol rosé was given us by Lucien Peyraud during a memorable visit to Domaine Tempier.

'Don't worry, my car knows the way by itself,' said Monsieur Peyraud, swinging the steering wheel and slamming the gears of his beat-up old 2-CV, as we climbed to the terraced *restanques* of one of his vineyards (he has four). 'I make my rosé from vines which are less than ten years old. That makes it lighter. Although it's a strong 13.5°, it doesn't knock you out. And I never, never add sugar.' Monsieur Peyraud was shocked that this habit had been allowed in the sunny south, which shouldn't need it, and where formerly it was strictly forbidden. 'A lot of wines are getting into a class they don't belong to – unnaturally.'

We were on a red clay hill 1,300 feet above Mediterranean level near the fortress of Le Beausset, looking onto a valley of vineyards winding down towards Bandol, the ancient port which shipped wine to the French colonies. Somewhere about 600BC the Greeks are reckoned to have brought the vine to this coast, and Bandol was already active in Roman times. Domaine Tempier was started in 1854 by a family of Marseilles tanners. Lucien Peyraud, native of St-Etienne, a town noted for its energy, married into the family and is still very much its head – with two sons, five daughters and fourteen grandchildren.

Beneath the bougainvillaea of a shady terrace, we were greeted by vivacious Lucienne Peyraud (née Tempier), known as Lucie. It was a riotous lunch. Even before aperitifs were over, Carey was photographing our hosts on an enormous sofa among the exquisite bibelots of the *salon*. It was a room of sun and shady corners, flowers and laughter, the kind of room where I imagined Colette would be very much at home.

We were shown the kitchen where Lucie had cooked our lunch. The nineteenth-century *batterie de cuisine* was still intact and very much in use. 'Lucien told me to make lunch Provençal,' she said. 'Well, I'm Marseillaise. I exaggerate everything, so lunch today is very, *very* Provençal.' First came marinaded sardines, then leg of lamb with olives, red peppers, and aubergines, Banon goat's cheese, and melon with the homemade dessert wine of Provence, *vin cuit*.

'The moment you put the right dish with the right wine,' Monsieur Peyraud said, 'you have a good tasting. A metabolization takes place. Try this '81 now – a big year, just ready to be drunk with lamb. Taste it before and after you eat, and see the difference.'

Cassis bay

The Peyraud Kitchen

The red was made with the single-grape *cépage*, Mourvèdre, strong in alcohol, the colour of garnet, smooth and well-bred, with a taste of crushed, ripe fruit. And many other subtleties beyond my palate.

Lucien Peyraud gave us this tasting lesson without the least pomposity and with much mirth. He hates show-off wine buffery: even experts had different palates; what one discovered, the other couldn't, all in the same wine. My head was reeling with all this good food, wine, and knowledge. At a lunch tasting like this, there was naturally nowhere to spit, and it was hard to refuse any of this superb wine. The convivial experience lasted several hours, and we came away feeling that, if wine gave *joie de vivre*, the Peyraud family were its living proof.

Domaine Tempier, Bandol

Lucien Peyraud proposes a toast

There could not be two more different makers of red wine than traditionalist Lucien Peyraud of Domaine Tempier and revolutionary Georges Brunet of Château Vignelaure, near Rians. But both agree on one thing: good wine is best drunk with good food.

Georges Brunet, owner of the Italianate château of Vignelaure since 1970, proudly showed us his extraordinary red-carpeted cellar. Red-carpeted, because it also served as an art gallery for his private collection. 'Many artists and writers are my friends,' he told us. 'So I ask them to do labels for my wines. Look, here's one written by Anthony Burgess: *When I drink the wines of*

Georges and Catherine Brunet
tasting Château Vignelaure 1986

Vignelaure, I hear violins. . . . He even composed a little music to go on the label too!' Art among the oak barrels: photographs by Henri Cartier-Bresson, sculpture by César, a Bernard Buffet Crucifixion. 'Must be worth a good three hundred thousand francs by now,' Monsieur Brunet continued. 'Naturally I paid Bernard one or two bottles for it.' That was his system of barter: art for wine's sake.

We were getting late for lunch, and friends were waiting on the terrace. And Catherine Brunet, *soignée* in country Chanel, greeted us beneath a great lime tree, where a table was set for lunch.

Cicadas sang and lime-blossom gently showered us, as we were treated to figs and prosciutto, stuffed lamb with whole roast garlic cloves and green beans, goat's cheese, and an apricot ice cream pudding (layers of apricots, peaches, and pistachio). 'By our friend, Roger Vergé,' said Madame Brunet. Another masterpiece.

'Wine follows wealth,' said Monsieur Brunet, discreetly tasting the wine the butler had poured. 'Like everything beautiful.' We moved from the purple '85 to the slightly paler '82. 'It's a disagreeable aspect of wine and art.' From the '82 to the great year of '79, we sniffed and sipped on.

Meanwhile the expansive, art-loving *vigneron* told us of his revolution. As a change from the heavy fruitiness of Côtes-du-Rhône, he had set out to make a less strong, lighter Midi red which had finesse, elegance, and nuance. After a long fight with the Coteaux d'Aix powers-that-be, this former owner of the Bordeaux Château La Lagune was allowed to cut down his traditional Grenache to ten per cent, bring in sixty per cent Cabernet-Sauvignon ('my Bordeaux experience') and thirty per cent Syrah ('the great Rhône grape of Tain l'Hermitage'). The last two grapes, he believed, made the best balanced wine. 'But I'm not just making a Midi claret,' he stressed. 'The red soil here is what gives my wine its own personality.' Moving from the '79 to the light, tawny '72, I knew what he meant; revolutionary winemaking in the land of Mirabeau had the taste of victory.

'But do most wine drinkers appreciate originality?' I asked. 'No, most want conformity,

Château Vignelaure, Rians

Cassis vineyards

something they instantly recognize as the same, year in, year out. How boring! Champagne? Ugh. Stuffed with chemicals to make it taste the same. Even the big firms do it.'

As we said goodbye, Georges Brunet talked of sweeping changes at Vignelaure, thanks to a shot of finance from a New Jersey hotelier – new offices, bigger cellars, greater thrust for Vignelaure in the markets of the world. 'My Americans are quite capable of doing it with me. And quite capable of not doing it. One never knows, does one?'

Exactly. Like the way of wine – one never knows how its mysterious, inexplicable evolution in vat and bottle will turn out. As Lucien Peyraud said in his *chai*, as we toured the vats: 'This is where the great mystery happens. We do all we can, then it's up to nature. We wait – and taste.'

SOME WINES OF OUR REGION

Including those mentioned in this chapter, here are the winemakers whose vintages we have most enjoyed. Worth looking out for on wine lists or if you happen to be driving this way.

Côtes-du-Rhône Villages Cave Coopérative de Visan, Clos du Père Clement (Visan), Domaine La Cantharide (Visan), Domaine du Val des Rois (Valréas), Domaine des Grands Devers (Valréas), Château d' Estagnol (Suze-la-Rousse), Le Petit Barbaras (Bouchet), Caveau Chantécotes (Ste-Cécile-des-Vignes), La Présidente (Ste-Cécile des Vignes), Rabasse-Charavin (Cairanne), Domaine Ste-Anne (St-Gervais), Jean Vinson (Vinsobres), Jean Courtois (Vinsobres), Domaine des Girasols (Roaix), Domaine St-Claude (Vaison-la- Romaine).

Châteauneuf-du-Pape Château de Beaucastel, Domaine du Vieux Télégraphe, Clos des Papes.

Others Cave Coopérative de Vaison-la-Romaine (for Côtes-du-Ventoux), Cave Coopérative de Puyméras (for white), Domaine de Grangeneuve (at Roussas, for Coteaux du Tricastin rosé), Castaud Maurin (for Muscat de Beaumes-de-Venise).

Further afield Domaine de Régusse (near Manosque), Château Vignelaure (Rians), Domaine Tempier (Bandol), Clos Ste-Magdeleine (Cassis).

Cassis waterfront

BIRDS, BEASTS,
AND BANGS

A delicate pig never got fat.
PROVENÇAL PROVERB

There is a very good reason why delicate pigs in Provence never get fat; in their delicate state, they absent-mindedly wander into an autumn wood and get shot. Which is the fate of anything that moves, once the hunting season begins.

In spring I have seen a brace of pheasants making love on our lane; in summer Carey and I encountered six wild boar hell-bent on destroying a chestnut wood, not ten yards off a main road

Pierrot Ramour leads the hunt in the Drôme hills

Hunting lodge, Montréal

near Banon; but come autumn, just when they're wanted, all game seems unsportingly absent. Where are the hare, thrush and partridge? The roebuck and woodcock? Quail and turtledove? Snipe, kid and plovers? Can it be the sheer frustration of never sighting any of these prizes, reckoned all to be fair game in Provence, that makes the hunters so trigger-happy?

Vineyard owner Pierrot Ramour, a keen hunter, says this is just an Englishman's view of French rough shooting with scarcer prey, because we are spoilt by driven birds falling from the skies like flies. 'In Britain,' Pierrot said, 'the game comes to you. In France, we go to the game. That's the difference. More sporting? I didn't say that. What's sporting about killing animals anyway? It's just an excuse for a good day with friends in the open air.'

And, as I found out, some Rabelaisian carousing into the bargain.

Up at five a.m. on a chilly November morning. And soon stirred from lethargy by a loud honking horn and rock music blaring from a car's cassette-player. This pre-dawn burst of country energy was Pierrot and his eighteen-year-old son, Pierre, come to pick us up in a red four-wheel-drive Toyota. In the back the beagles: Hugo, Vodka, Perlette, Horry, Maya, Oscar, Nenette and Dino. And the guns, correctly broken for road transport. Exemplary law-abiding behaviour; for three years Pierrot had been Visan's *garde de chasse*, seeing to it that, among other things, no one shot near a house or a road without their back to it.

We headed for the Drôme hills, to a private rough shoot on sheep farmer's land near the upland village of Montréal. After heavy night rain, the Toyota skidded and whined on a slippery mountain road with precipitous drops. It was a relief to reach the hunting lodge, a Union Jack had been hoisted in our honour, and we were welcomed by Pierrot's fellow-hunters: the lodge's owner, Kinou Bartheye, executive at a nearby winery; and black-moustachioed Chanet Le Franc, a big bear of a man who worked at the Visan Mairie. It was just getting light. Bitterly cold. Thawing out by a blazing log fire, we drank steaming black coffee and cognac, provided by Kinou's wife Françoise. The shooting party was on.

We set out for the plateau. The beagles tried to pick up scents. 'Damn wind!' complained Chanet. 'It's blowing the scents away.' We reached the little valley of Combe, where wild boar and pheasant were alleged to be. Then the sun came up from behind the mountains, making red cheeks redder but hearts warmer. The hunters spread out, communicating with walkie-talkies.

A weird figure attached himself to our group, a local Monsieur Know-It-All dressed in black, who carried a gun and spoke wildly. 'I seen a wild boar!' 'Where?' 'Down there in the chestnut wood!' 'Show us then.' 'Oh, he won't be there now.' 'Thanks for the help!'

Eight-thirty and still no game. Monsieur Know-It-All was still hanging in there, driving the hunters mad with advice about his wild boar. Only the dogs seemed to like him, sniffing round him as if about to pee on his tattered black pants. The hunters decided to go to another place altogether, where there could be hares.

Hare sighted! A commando approach was devised, young Pierre sent up on to a ridge, his father Pierrot below, with the dogs in between. 'Putain de vent!' Pierrot swore. Again the bitter wind carried away the scent.

We reached a lonely farm. Mangy black dogs leapt madly at us from chains, snarling and baring teeth. The farmer and his wife hadn't seen anyone for two weeks. Suddenly, gunfire from nearby. Our dogs' barking joined that of the mad dogs of the farm. More shots, nearer this time. And out of the bushes ran a rabbit. Young Pierre shot it dead.

Small rabbit, big battle. It was twelve o'clock. 'Sometimes we go on till two,' said Kinou. 'Not today,' said Pierrot, hastily adding: 'There's too much wind. Let's eat.'

Back at the lodge, the day's festivities began in earnest. We were treated as honoured guests, and the day's hunting seemed a mere preliminary to the ensuing feast. A smell of woodsmoke and pheasant roasting on a spit welcomed us. 'When you've killed something,' Pierrot said, 'you feel good because you can eat. Then, over the meal, the whole strategy of the kill can be discussed – like a mini-war.'

Not much strategy talk that day, however. The bag had been just a few rabbits and hares, but nobody really cared. After all the biting fresh air and stomping about steep hillsides, it was time to get up a good fug and gratify the senses with food and drink.

The hunt lunch began. Each person had brought two courses to share with the others: apart from the two spit-roast pheasants, there were kidneys in garlic sauce, salad of curly lettuce, cardoons (an edible thistle, beloved of Provençals in winter) in béchamel sauce, thrush pâté, wild boar stew, goat's cheese, peach wine, Côtes-du-Rhône, and a verbena liqueur.

The red wine had come from five different wineries, and each man boasted the merits of

Practising bird calls

what he'd bought. 'Try this!' someone said, pulling a cork, bottle between his knees. Silence. Tasting all round. *'Dégueulasse!'* said another, making a sickened face. 'Wait till you've tasted mine!' So the wine-joshing went on till all five bottles had been roundly praised, insulted, and consumed. And more appeared.

Then began the silly anecdotes. One of the hunters, a road-mender, said: 'The other day I crushed a snail. I just couldn't stand it following me any more!' Then there was poetry reading: Mistral, naturally – in the original Provençal. Verses describing a hunter who had shot a nightingale were greeted with high emotion. *'Le salaud!'* Chanet shouted, tears rolling down his cheeks. 'Just let me get my hands on a hunter who could shoot a nightingale!'

Then came the bird whistles, each with a different call. Carey had to hold a long note and looked fit to burst. It was cabaret time. Funny hats, bawdy songs, dressing up in drag. The songs

got bawdier. 'Get your camera ready, Carey!' Pierrot said, in a state of excited complicity. 'Don't miss this one.' Kinou made an entrance, cheeks rouged and lips reddened, wearing Françoise's long tee-shirt, and sang a song with a quick-flash pay-off – too quick for Carey's camera, unfortunately.

But the real climax of the show was the thrilling, never-to-be-forgotten drama of the drive back down that perilous mountain track. Unfortunately I cannot report on it, for my eyes were tight closed. Whether in fear or drunken sleep can remain my secret.

That memorable hunting day, we had only seen one rabbit actually bite the dust. But rabbit is always welcome, one of the great favourites of the Provençals – *Lapin aux aromates* (marinaded in herbs), *Paquetons de lapin* (herb-flavoured pieces

Pheasants on the spit

104

Hunters' lunch

Vinsobres

wrapped in bacon), and *Civet de lapin* (casserole cooked in wine and herbs). The last is more luxuriously done with hare, in the manner of English jugged hare but including an elaborate marinade and the hare's blood. Less earthy and more delicate is Marie-Anne Founès' *Lapin surprise à la provençale*.

In the kitchen of L'Auberge de Reillanne, I watched her carefully boning the young rabbit, assisted by a Moroccan and a girl from Boston. It was like watching a master-craftsman with eager apprentices; attention was total. Yet Marie-Anne's touch was always light: cooking, in her view, also had its comedy; often chefs were too inhuman and humourless. 'My Surprise Rabbit,' she explained, 'is something I have to do in advance. I can't be taken by surprise myself, so it's not on the menu. Just for special guests who order it.'

Specialities of Marie-Anne's are a Pigeon Salad with Baked Pears, Breast of Duck with Sesame and Three Fruits (dried fig, red currant, and raspberry vinegar), and Guinea Fowl with Peaches. Her mixture of birds and fruit of Provence is far from chichi: down-to-earth but elegant, like the prose of Jean Giono.

For the less ambitious, let me recommend *Salmis de faisan* or *Perdreaux aux lentilles*, both impressive to serve and relatively easy to cook. Or, my own more basic winged speciality which requires no skill with gun and very little in the kitchen either, Garlic Chicken, roasted with forty-five cloves of garlic. House-guests, pale from northern rigours, go a good deal paler when they hear what's for dinner; but it only takes one bite of the subtly impregnated chicken flesh, and the puréed garlic oozing from crisply roasted cloves, for them to be instantly converted.

Heavier game, the Wild Boar Stews and Spit-Roasted Kid, is best left to professionals like Charles Mouret of the St-Hubert, Entrechaux. His is the third generation to own the restaurant; unfortunately game in Provence is not as plentiful as it once was. This other flight from the land has in no way diminished the Provençal love of game dishes, and Monsieur Mouret travels once every two weeks in winter to Alsace, the one region of France where deer, kid, wild boar, pheasant and partridge are still sufficiently abundant to meet a busy restaurateur's requirements.

Pheasant, partridge, duck and wild boar in the larder of the St-Hubert Restaurant

SALMIS DE FAISAN

Ragout of pheasant. Recipe of Monsieur Mouret of the St-Hubert, Entrechaux. Serves 4.

1 young pheasant
1oz/30g raw ham or lean bacon, diced
12 juniper berries
2–3 tbs olive oil
1 tbs brandy
1oz/30g carrot, diced
1oz/30g onion, diced
celery leaves, chopped
thyme
½ clove garlic, chopped
40ml white wine
stock
4 slices bread
slices of truffle (optional)

Take the legs and breasts of the pheasant (reserving the carcase), and, in a frying pan, seize them in olive oil with ham and juniper berries. Reduce heat a little. Turn, so that they are golden brown all over. Keep frying until the blood does not run when pieces are pricked with a fork. Take out and flambé with brandy. Keep pheasant warm and covered.

Break up the carcase with poultry scissors and put in the same pan with the remaining juices, adding onion, carrot, celery, garlic and thyme. Brown all these ingredients, taking care not to burn. Add wine and déglacé pan. Reduce to about half quantity by cooking on. Then add stock to cover contents. Cover pan, putting a large circle of greaseproof paper under the lid to cut down on evaporation. Simmer for 30 minutes.

Lift out bones. Purée the rest of the contents in mixer or processor or fine plate of a vegetable mill, to make sauce. Cover and simmer gently for 10 minutes. Only now season with pepper – probably no salt will be needed. If too thin add about 100ml cream and stir until sauce thickens.

Fry the bread and put a piece under each piece of pheasant in the serving dish. Lay the (optional) truffle slices on top and spoon the sauce over the dish. Serve with apples which have been cored and filled with red currant jelly and baked in the oven.

POULET À L'AIL AU RIZ

Garlic chicken with rice. Our own recipe. Serves 6.

5lb/2¼kg free-range roasting chicken, with liver
1 shallot, chopped
chunk of stale bread
45 cloves garlic unpeeled
handfuls of all fresh herbs available
4 tbs/60ml olive oil
salt and pepper
1 onion, chopped
2 tbs/30ml double (heavy) cream
10½oz/300g (1¼ cups) brown long-grain rice
1½ pints/900ml (3¾ cups) stock or water
3 tomatoes, peeled, seeded and chopped

Put chicken liver to simmer for 20 minutes in a little salted water with chopped shallot.

Rub bread with 4–5 cut cloves garlic. Push herbs inside chicken, filling cavity with garlic bread. Skewer or sew chicken to close it. In roasting pan, put 3 tbs olive oil, the other 40 garlic cloves (less if you must!), and the chicken seasoned and massaged with olive oil. Roast in oven, pre-heated to 400°F/200°C/Gas Mark 6, for 30 minutes, turning and basting with hot water so garlic does not burn. Reduce heat for further 30 minutes and test if chicken is cooked.

Meanwhile, in a large frying pan (skillet) fry onion in 1 tbs olive oil till soft. Add rice, turning it all until shining and golden. Add 1½ pint/900ml (3¾cups) salted water and boil gently about 15 minutes or until cooked. Stir in tomatoes and keep warm.

Open up the chicken, take out garlic bread, cut in slices and spread with mashed chicken liver. Throw away herbs. Place carved chicken and garlic on serving dish, pile bread on top and keep warm.

Make sauce by adding cream to roasting juices with a little stock if sauce is too thick; pass this round separately. Serve all very hot, each person taking some garlic bread to squash the creamy inside out of the roasted garlic skins.

PERDREAUX AUX LENTILLES

This recipe for partridge with lentils is from Madame Latour of Domaine de la Cabasse, Séguret. The chicken stock is best made from the bones and wing tips, flavoured with bay leaves and basil. Serves 4.

1 large onion, chopped
1oz/25g (2 tbs) butter
1lb/450g green lentils
1 wine glass white wine
2 pints/1 litre chicken stock
salt and pepper to taste
2 sprigs thyme
4 chicken livers
2 roasting partridges, without liver or giblets
2 tbs/30ml groundnut oil
1 tsp/5ml wine vinegar

FOR THE CROÛTONS

8 small slices white bread
2 cloves garlic, peeled and halved
4oz/100g ($\frac{1}{2}$ cup) butter

In a flame-proof casserole, soften the onion in butter without browning. Add the uncooked lentils, wine and stock. Simmer gently for at least 1 hour or until lentils are cooked. Season with salt and pepper.

Put a sprig of thyme and 2 chicken livers inside each partridge, and put them in a casserole with a thick base in which you have first put the groundnut oil. Let them take colour, turning often, then cover and pot roast them gently for about 30 minutes, basting every 5 minutes.

When the thighs are pricked with a fork and the juice runs clear, they are done. With poultry scissors or a meat cleaver, cut them in two, up the breastbone and the backbone, to make 4 halves. Keep warm. Put the livers aside.

To make the croûtons, rub the slices of bread with the garlic halves, then fry gently in the butter.

With the vinegar deglaze the casserole in which the partridges were roasted, and mash the livers into this mixture to make a thick cream. Spread this on the garlic croûtons.

Serve on a wide dish, making a bed of the lentils, with the croûtons on top and the partridge halves on top of them.

LAPIN SURPRISE À LA PROVENÇALE

*Provençal rabbit surprise. Recipe of Madame Founès, of
L'Auberge de Reillanne. Serves 2.*

2 large green and 2 large red peppers, bell-shaped
2 small wild rabbits, boned, with livers
(use hind quarters only)
1 tsp/5ml each fresh thyme, savory, rosemary, crushed bay-leaves
3 tbs Meaux mustard (with seeds)
salt and pepper
2 tbs/30ml olive oil
2 tbs/30ml thin (pouring) cream

Cut tops off peppers. Clean out seeds carefully. Chop liver and mix
with the herbs and mustard. Season rabbit pieces and insides of
peppers with salt and pepper. Roll rabbit pieces in herb and mustard
mixture and pack all into the peppers. Put red caps on green peppers,
green caps on red peppers and tie with kitchen string.

Put olive oil in baking tin (pan), pack peppers closely and sprinkle
with more oil. Bake in pre-heated hot oven, 450°F/230°C/Gas Mark
8, for 30 minutes, basting with hot water occasionally. After 15
minutes cover with foil. Put cooked peppers on serving dish and keep
warm.

Make a sauce by adding cream to roasting juices, pour the sauce
over the peppers and serve with rice. (Madame Founès uses
Camargue brown round-grain or Uncle Ben's brown long-grain,
always allowing rice to take colour in olive oil with a little onion
before boiling.)

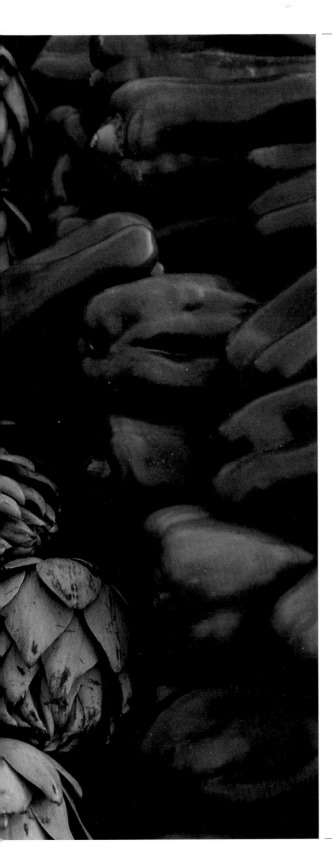

Artichokes and peppers

MARKET DAY

Oh! Garlic, and sweet white sugary onions, aubergine and basil. Just saying their names is a song.
COLETTE, LETTER TO FRANCIS POULENC

As though calling firemen to an emergency, a siren's worrying cry crescendoed into the morning air. Odd for a Provençal market. Not at all like our familiar market at Vaison-la-Romaine, where a Barbary organ or wandering choristers from the choir festival make sweeter sounds.

But this was no familiar market. This was Châteaurenard in the heart of Provence's Big Vegetable and Fruit Country, the rich alluvial plain of the Durance river. And bigger than that markets do not come: it is the largest in Europe. In a top floor room of the Hôtel Phec, where we had been invited for a birds-eye view of the market's thirty-two acres, the kindly proprietor, Monsieur

Market at
Châteaurenard

Copiatti, put our minds at rest about the siren: 'It signals the beginning of trading in various categories. Aubergine buyers and sellers wait for the 7.30 siren, for instance; before that, it's forbidden to trade.'

The action reminded me more of a race meeting than a market. Row upon row of vans and trucks; huddles of men discussing 'form', impatient for the 'off'; constantly relayed messages and instructions over the PA system; the sheer open-air vastness of the event. It was just coming up to 6.30, time for the first 'race' – melons.

Growers on the melon row stood by trucks piled high with freshly picked melons. I have never seen more melons in my life; their pervasive, sweet perfume was everywhere about us. The siren sounded, and the race was on: a mere fifteen minutes to trade the melons. Wholesale buyers dashed about, arguing, making notes, appraising the fruit with the eye of the expert, like art-dealers at Sothebys. Soon it would be the turn of the next row. I studied my 'race-card': 6.45 tomatoes; 7.00 fruit with stones; 7.15 fruit with pips; 7.30 vegetables (aubergines, peppers, courgettes); 7.45 haricot beans.

In winter, of course, the 'races' are different; 7.00 sales by sample (e.g. greenhouse lettuce); 7.15 *frisée* and *scarole* lettuce, leeks, parsley, radish; 7.30 spinach, potatoes; 7.45 cauliflowers.

Blue-sky travel posters of Provence are misleading; the weather is much more seasonally extreme than one imagines, and an icy mistral can arrive at any time of year. But somehow the blessed southern climate always comes through, delivering the earliest produce of the year – *primeurs*, the pride of the region. Last year 400,000 tons of *primeurs* left Châteaurenard market on their way to London, Paris, Amsterdam – destinations all over Europe.

Outside the market's compound, juggernaut trucks waited at the loading-bays and would soon be headed north on the *autoroute*. But today there was something rotten in the state of Châteaurenard, and it certainly wasn't the aubergines. The market gardeners' union were handing out leaflets, complaining of unfair competition from Spain since its arrival in the Common Market. 'It's a bad moment,' said Monsieur Lantelme, grower of beans, fennel, cauliflower and mandarin oranges in his greenhouse. 'Especially for young market gardeners with a heavy

Market at Nyons

loan from the Crédit Agricole. My sons are wise – they're both bakers! Trouble is, the Spaniards go for quantity rather than quality – and, unfortunately, quantity's what our supermarkets want.'

Pictures of overturned, charred Spanish trucks, victims of French farmers' violent protest, seemed far removed from the brisk, good-humoured trading that morning. A joker, seeing Carey's camera, had placed two tomatoes and a huge courgette in phallic display on his truck, and shouted: '*Ma pouce*, take it at a better angle than that!' The *garde* was another joke: his thankless task was to stop people dealing outside the laid-down hours, and fat chance he had of enforcing it. 'Stand by your truck!' he shouted, and a grower obeyed with mock meekness. But as soon as the *garde* moved on, the grower blew a raspberry, and the wholesale buyer gave me a lawless wink.

If Monsieur Lantelme is right, and the quality of this superb, unbelievably fresh produce is under threat, whether from over-production, non-competitive prices or whatever, it is sad indeed. Châteaurenard is enough to turn hardened meat-eaters into vegetarians; everywhere were the perfect ingredients of our favourite dishes. Mound upon mound of glistening peppers, aubergines or courgettes for Provence's renowned Stuffed Vegetables – or for a Gratin of Courgettes with Rice on Aubergines with Tomatoes; an entire vanload of basil, whose sweet smell drowned the fumes of departing trucks, for Fresh Basil in Olive Oil (a winter preserve); string upon string of fresh young garlic for Fresh Roast Garlic; bulb upon bulb of fennel for Fennel with Tomato. And tomatoes, tomatoes all the way. . . .

By nine o'clock, market gardeners who had been in their allotted parking spaces at five (later arrival would cause a traffic back-up from here to

Monsieur Rippert's tomatoes near Châteaurenard

Avignon) were already back at work. Many did not have far to go. Not more than a kilometre to the north, between the market and the Durance, are literally hundreds of market gardens, irrigated by a sophisticated system of channels. Growers can flood orchards – after putting down fertilizer, for instance – from channels which come directly from the Durance.

On *Le Chemin des Digues* (Road of the Dykes) we met Monsieur Rippert, tomato grower, just back from market, already busy organizing the rest of his day on the phone in his pick-up truck. It was our day for 'the biggest ever', and now it was the turn of the biggest-ever greenhouse: more than $2\frac{1}{2}$ acres of glass which yielded enough tomatoes to take truckloads to market every two days. High-tech ventilation for the big heat of summer had the automated glass roof sections opening and closing by thermostatic control.

Not all vegetable-growing is on such a massive

scale. Monsieur Bernard of Visan, officially retired, works three *potagers*, small kitchen gardens, on a casual share-cropping basis, paying no rent but providing the owners with a carrot or two now and again. 'Like for my son-in-law's relations. They're too old to garden, and they don't want some *hurluberlu* of a gardener. I'm like a friend, helping out.' He was being excessively modest. Monsieur Bernard's range covered things I did not see even at Châteaurenard – *blettes, mange-touts, cornichons*, whose English translations are respectively spinach beet (or Swiss chard), sugar pea (string beans in the States), and gherkins (smaller than Polish).

Monsieur Bernard's speciality is asparagus. That morning, he dug some out for us with a special long tool from the mounds of earth he had made over the plants in January. First shoots are dug out in March and continue to arrive until the plants 'rest' – after the Valréas festival of Petit St-Jean at the end of June. For us, tasting Monsieur

Pastrycook at L'Oustau de Baumanière

Horse sale, Apt market

Bernard's asparagus, all that exacting work was certainly worth while. But for him? *'Ah, oui, oui, oui!'* he answered unhesitatingly.

Such asparagus deserves to be eaten by itself, boiled or steamed, with a vinaigrette or melted butter. But near us there is an *auberge paysanne* – a country inn – to which people come from miles around for Madame Roux's Asparagus in a Béchamel Sauce. L'Auberge de Pontillard at Piègon announces asparagus for sale, so you can be sure that it has come to your plate fresh from the ground that morning.

That applies to certain very special green beans, too. 'I will plunge into the beans for you,' said Monsieur Llorens, in charge of the kitchen garden of L'Oustau de Baumanière. 'Everything you see is organic. No chemicals. It costs the *patron* a fortune.' Monsieur Llorens plunged into the baby green beans, and emerged with a handful. 'See how tiny they are? They do not even grow a day. Picked in the morning and eaten at lunchtime.'

Midday. All was calm and confident in the restaurant kitchen, as Jean-André Charial and his staff of eighteen prepared lunch. A *pâtissier* was taking tarts from the pastry oven; a girl crushed coffee beans for ice cream; a boy squeezed oranges for a Bucks Fizz in a corner; and two teams of six were fully employed, topping and tailing Monsieur Llorens' baby green beans, so tiny they are known as 'angel's hair beans'. . . .

'I've seen that being done for eighteen years,' said Jean André, and added with typical modesty: 'I've changed things a bit since I started. But not much. You know my grandfather, don't you?' Casually he introduced us to the Grand Old Man of Provençal gastronomy, the venerable Raymond Thuilier, still in his kitchen every day. In spite of world-wide fame, it felt still very much like a family restaurant; we were welcomed into that holy of holies, its kitchen, like old friends, given the freedom of the house even at its busiest time.

Then, out on to the terrace for lunch. Only a few hours ago, those beans had been on the vine. Finer and fresher they do not come. But anywhere in Provence they are a joy, and plain steaming or boiling is not the only way to serve them.

LÉGUMES FARCIS

A classic recipe for stuffed vegetables. Serves 6–8.

8 tomatoes
8 red/green peppers (bell-shaped)
4 small aubergines (eggplants)
4 medium courgettes (zucchini)
2 tbs/30ml olive oil

STUFFING

3 tbs/45ml olive oil
1 large onion, chopped
2 slices bread
$\frac{1}{4}$ pint/150ml ($\frac{2}{3}$ cup) milk
$3\frac{1}{2}$oz/100g ($\frac{1}{2}$ cup) lean bacon or sausage meat
3 cloves garlic, crushed
1 crumbled bay leaf
handful chopped parsley
2 eggs, beaten
2oz/50g ($\frac{2}{3}$ cup) grated cheese
breadcrumbs
stock, to baste
salt and pepper

Cut tops off tomatoes, remove seeds and drain. Spoon out some of flesh and reserve (tomato shells are now ready for stuffing). Cut tops off peppers, remove seeds. Cut aubergines (eggplants) and courgettes (zucchini) in half longways. Carefully spoon out flesh and reserve, leaving firm shells. Cook pepper, courgettes (zucchini) and aubergine (eggplant) shells in olive oil until soft but not collapsing.

For the stuffing, heat oil and soften onion. Soak bread in milk and squeeze out. Chop flesh of vegetables finely. Add these and all other ingredients except eggs, cheese and stock. Cook together gently for about 10 minutes.

Arrange vegetable shells closely in a wide oven dish. Take stuffing off heat, quickly stir in eggs and cheese. Season. Fill vegetables, including uncooked tomatoes, with stuffing and replace tomato caps. Sprinkle with breadcrumbs, dot with butter or olive oil, surround with stock, and leave in slow oven, 325°F/170°C/Gas Mark 3, for at least 1 hour. Baste often so dish does not dry out.

Good hot and even better cold.

TOMATES À LA PROVENÇALE

The traditional Provençal way of cooking tomatoes takes longer than just a few minutes in the frying pan (skillet).

FOR EACH PERSON

2 ripe tomatoes
1 tbs/15ml olive oil
salt
½ tsp/2.5ml sugar
½ clove garlic, chopped
1 tbs/15ml chopped chervil

Cut tomatoes across, de-seed and drain off liquid. Heat olive oil in a heavy frying pan (skillet), put the tomatoes in open side downwards and cook very gently for 45 minutes, moving them around from time to time. Turn them over carefully, add salt, sugar, garlic, chervil and a few drops of olive oil to each one. Leave to cook for the same length of time again, when they will be different from any tomatoes you have ever tasted.

GRATIN DE COURGETTES AU RIZ

Gratin of courgettes (zucchini) and rice. Recipe of Madame Campdorasse of Grimaud. Serves 6.

4 tbs/60ml olive oil
2 large onions, chopped
2 cloves garlic, chopped
2lb/900g small firm courgettes (zucchini), cut in ⅜in/1cm slices
1 bay leaf
2oz/50g (3 tbs) long-grain rice
1 egg
2oz/50g (⅔ cup) grated Parmesan/Gruyère cheese
salt and pepper, to taste

Heat the oil in a thick pan, cook the onion and garlic till soft but not brown. Add courgettes (zucchini) and bay leaf, and cook on till tender. Boil rice for 10 minutes. Add to courgettes (zucchini) with beaten egg, most of cheese, salt and pepper.

Put in oiled oven dish, sprinkle with olive oil and the rest of the cheese, and bake for about 25 mins in moderate oven, 350°F/180°C/Gas Mark 4. Then raise heat for 10 minutes to make top crusty brown.

HARICOTS VERTS À LA PROVENÇALE

Green beans as prepared in Provence. Serves 4.

1lb/450g green beans
4 tomatoes, skinned and chopped
1 onion, chopped
1 tbs/15ml olive oil
½ clove garlic
1 tsp/5ml savory
1 tsp/5ml each chopped parsley and basil

Blanch green beans in boiling water for 4–5 minutes, then rinse in cold water. Fry tomatoes and onion lightly in olive oil. Add crushed garlic and savory. Leave to reduce, covered, over gentle heat. Add green beans and cook for 15 minutes.

Serve with chopped parsley and basil.

FRESH BASIL OR TARRAGON IN OLIVE OIL

To preserve for winter. Very good with a tomato salad in mid-winter to remind one of summer.

Pick fistfuls of basil leaves at the height of the season, wash and pat dry. Pound with pestle and mortar to a broken-down state, but not a paste. Pack jars half full of leaves and fill up with olive oil. Store in fridge. Keep for two months before using.

Fresh tarragon (for winter roast chicken, for example) can also be similarly preserved, but a few sprigs only are enough to impregnate the oil.

ASPERGES À LA BÉCHAMEL

Asparagus in Béchamel sauce. Recipe of Madame Roux of L'Auberge de Pontillard, Piègon. Serves 6.

1lb/450g asparagus (need not be the thick kind)
1oz/25g butter
1oz/25g flour
¾pt/1½ cups milk
¼pt/½ cup chicken stock (or cube)
salt and pepper
nutmeg
2 tbs fresh cream
handful Gruyère cheese, grated

Clean, scrape, and boil the asparagus till just tender. Discard any hard bits, cut the rest in short pieces.

Make a white sauce with the butter, flour, boiled milk and chicken stock. Season and add a little grated nutmeg. Stir in cream.

Turn asparagus carefully in the sauce. Put in oiled oven dish, sprinkle with Gruyère and bake for about 30 minutes at 375°F/190°C/Gas Mark 5 until top is golden and bubbling.

FENOUILS À LA TOMATE

Fennel and tomatoes. Serves 4–6.

2 big onions, cut in quarters
2 tbs/30ml olive oil
5oz/150g (⅔ cup) diced streaky bacon (or lean belly of pork)
6 fennel bulbs, cut in quarters
6 cloves garlic
4fl oz/100ml (½ cup) white wine
6 tomatoes, peeled and seeded (or 1 large can)
salt and pepper
2 bay leaves

Soften quartered onions in oil, add bacon dice and cook 5 minutes. Add fennel and cook 10 minutes turning them over. Add garlic and white wine. Continue cooking until reduced by half. Add tomatoes, salt, pepper and bay leaves. Simmer 1½ hours or until fennel is cooked.

GRATIN D'AUBERGINES À LA TOMATE

Gratin of aubergine (eggplant) and tomato. Our recipe. Serves 4–6.

3 medium aubergines (eggplants)
salt and pepper
4 tbs/60ml olive oil, or more
2 medium onions
¼ pint/150ml (⅔ cup) water
4 large tomatoes
1 large clove garlic
4fl oz/100ml (½ cup) white wine
2 tsp/10ml thyme
2 handfuls Parmesan cheese

Cut aubergines (eggplants) diagonally in slices ⅓in/1cm thick. Sprinkle with salt and leave to drain for 30 minutes. Pat dry, then fry in oil until golden. Drain on kitchen paper. Dice onions not too finely and fry in 1 tbs oil until soft. When oil is absorbed, add water and continue to cook until almost a purée (paste).

Slice tomatoes. Arrange slices of aubergine (eggplant) and tomato alternately in oiled gratin dish. Chop or crush garlic over dish and add white wine. Season with salt, pepper, and thyme leaves. Arrange onion purée over dish and sprinkle with Parmesan cheese. Bake in medium oven, 375°F/190°C/Gas Mark 5, for 30 minutes. Serve hot or cold.

Gratin d'aubergines à la tomate

Montjustin

MONSIEUR SEGUIN'S
CHEESE

'I want to go to the mountains, Monsieur Séguin.'
'But, you silly goat, don't you know the wolf is up there?
Suppose you met him. What would you do then?'
'I'd butt him with my horns, Monsieur Séguin.'
ALPHONSE DAUDET, 'MONSIEUR SÉGUIN'S GOAT'

At the St-Hubert, Entrechaux, Charles Mouret calls his goat's cheese salad *Salade Séguin*, and we all know what happened to that poor naïve creature. She got her freedom – and was eaten by the wolf for her pains.

Urban freedom-seekers who embark on the making of goat's cheese are taking almost as big a

Vauvenargues

gamble as Monsieur Séguin's goat. It is a tough life, as Marie-Anne Founès told me: 'My husband Florent and I gave' up being journalists in Paris, and moved into a beautiful old house on the Plan d'Albion above Apt. The simple life at 900 metres above sea level, bathed in the sweet light of Provence. Or so we thought.' That was in 1968, already a troubled enough year; the Founès should have known better than to start making goat's cheese in it. 'We had five years of passionate hell. Florent broke his back – literally. And we had to sell the business to a local restaurateur.'

Which proved to be lucky: the Founès fell in with the Gordes restaurant crowd, and she was taught to cook by a local culinary genius, Jean de Couteron, who regularly travelled between his own restaurant and theirs, giving free advice and helping them get started. 'We wanted to stay in Provence,' Florent said. 'So we took over L'Auberge de Reillanne.' And now the only reminders of the goat's cheese fiasco are pleasant ones: baking cheeses in the cinders of the dining-room fire in winter; and Marie-Anne's *Caillé de chèvre au concombre et à la menthe* (Creamy Goat's Cheese with Cucumber and Fresh Mint), an appropriately sweet-and-sour starter described later.

A few years ago, ecologically-minded young urbanites, fed up with city life, would take a three-month course in artisanal goat's cheese-making at Rambouillet, near Paris, and head for a new life in Provence. Usually they set up in couples; the pitfall was that one partner, daunted by the sheer hard work and failure to write the intended novel in the evenings, would drop out. The remaining partner would be forced to take on casual labour, and the genuinely high standard would fall. 'I don't trust the hygiene of some of that hippy cheese at Apt market,' said Claude Arnaud of St-Saturnin-d'Apt. 'As a restaurateur, I depend on consistent quality.'

Where would he go to find it? In the sparsely populated hills of Haute-Provence, you just have to ask around. If you can find anyone to ask. We had driven for kilometres on a winding hill road near Séderon, and had passed not a car, seen not a soul. Then we caught sight of a lone shepherd,

Jean Gilardi, Ongles

Drôme goatherd

Louis Chauvet, shepherd

Céreste

sitting under a pear tree, utterly at peace with himself and the world as he watched over his flock. Sheep, goats . . . Louis Chauvet knew all the flocks and herds for miles around, and could certainly tell you the best sheep farmer for lamb and the best goat farmer for cheese. Monsieur Chauvet seemed pleased to have a chat, even though it meant leaving the shade of his pear tree. According to Pierre Gleize, who knew him (everyone knows everyone where there is virtually no one), we were honoured; he was quite a character, Chauvet, very much a law unto himself, and known as *Le Baron du Trou*, because he ruled the little valley where his flocks grazed with almost feudal authority.

Last year he trained a German shepherdess, he told us. We thought he meant an Alsatian bitch, *berger allemand* being the name of that breed of dog in French. But in fact he was talking about a distinguished German surgeon's daughter, hooked on the outdoor life. Clearly she had seen him on German television; he has made several appearances in Europe, inspiring the middle-class young to dreams of lost peasant values and rebirth as shepherdess or cheese-maker.

Not everyone was so motivated by the eco-cult. Cheese-maker Jean Gilardi told me: 'We came here from Lyon, because our son had been ill and needed the mountain air.' The small Gilardi farm, nestling in a valley of herb-filled pastureland between Banon and Forcalquier, overlooks the majestic Montagne de Lure. They have thirty-one goats and make goat's cheese under the famous Banon label. The nature of the soil and herbs is particularly rich in that area, making gourmands even of the goats.

Jean and his wife, Mady, share the work. He looks after the goats, who never go further than five hundred metres from the house. 'There's plenty of good grazing within that distance, and they mustn't lose energy walking too much, or

Jean Gilardi's kid goats, Ongles

they don't make milk.' I had never thought of goats not walking; the comparatively sedentary life of a Banon goat is relieved by a good bout of butting.

It is a full year for the goats, however, as well as the Gilardis. In September the nannies are put with the billies. In February the kids are born. In March the milking season starts, and goes on till September. Then it all begins again.

Mady is in charge of the cheese-making. Up at five every day, an hour earlier than her husband, she starts by milking. Each day's milk waits twenty-four hours to sour. Then it is skimmed,

La Bonne Etape restaurant

and the resulting cheese put into pierced cartons to drain off the 'little' milk; left in a cold room for one month; wrapped in chestnut leaves; and delivered by Jean, in addition to his work with the goats, to shops and restaurants in the region, as far away as Manosque. It is also sold at the farm to passing tourists who specially appreciate certain cheeses containing pear liqueur and *eau-de-vie*.

Apart from the obvious problems of starting a new life, investment, and paying back loans, the worst frustration for the Gilardis is the idiotic lack of an *appellation contrôlée* for Banon. Picodon, the goat's cheese made between Valréas and Dieulefit, had its name and region of production protected – after twenty years of bureaucratic wrangling – so why not Banon? Even in a Banon grocery store, we saw a cheese on sale called Banon d'Or – made with cow's milk somewhere miles away in the Drôme! 'Wrap it in chestnut leaves,' said

Gilardi bitterly, 'and the dopes don't know the difference. It's a disgrace.'

The makers of Spanish Chablis and Irish Camembert would not agree. Nor, perhaps, would Messrs Leroy and Berger, cheese-makers at Malaucène. 'We're experimenting with a *camembert de chèvre* – making it with goat's milk, instead of cow's,' said Madame Leroy. 'It has the same crust, size and shape as Camembert, but it's much stronger. It's the taste of the Midi, but something different. Already we can't make enough!'

In the early days of their business, the Leroys would sometimes make too much. But it didn't go to waste, because they turned it into Cachat – a speciality of the region, and a simple recipe anyone can try.

Another of our favourites, made preferably with a goat cheese of strong, rich flavour (such as Picodon), is *Chèvre à l'huile*.

A choice of goat's cheese

CAILLÉ DE CHÈVRE AU CONCOMBRE ET À LA MENTHE

Creamy goat's cheese with cucumber and fresh mint. Recipe of Madame Founès of L'Auberge de Reillanne.

Caillé de chèvre is goat's cheese at its early liquid stage, which will not be easy to find. Use the softest possible goat's cheese and add fromage frais or thin cream, so that when you beat it together, the mixture has a good creamy consistency.

Serve onto individual plates. Add a swirl of runny, black oak honey (or acacia honey) in the middle. Encircle with thin slices of peeled cucumber and decorate with fresh mint leaves.

Madame Founès serves this as a starter, but it is also good as a dessert or cheese course.

CHÈVRE À L'HUILE

Goat's cheese in olive oil needs a strong-flavoured variety, but the flat picodons are the best. First prepare a large, wide-necked jar with a lid.

cheeses to fill the jar
3 or 4 sprigs each of thyme, savory, rosemary
8–10 black peppercorns
olive oil

Stack the cheeses in the jar. Push the herbs down the sides. Add peppercorns and fill with olive oil. Cover and keep a few weeks before using.

Serve with green salad or by itself with wholemeal bread (no butter).

LE CACHAT

Traditional recipe of the Malaucène area to use up broken goat's cheeses. This amount will be enough for several meals. Serve in small pots as it is very potent. Use approximately three parts goat's cheese to two parts fromage frais.

2 flat goat's cheeses
$\frac{2}{3}$ the weight of the cheese in fromage frais
(or cream or cottage cheese)
1 tsp/5ml olive oil
2 tsp/10ml savory or thyme
pepper, to taste
eau-de-vie or brandy to cover

Break up cheese with wooden spoon so there are no lumps, mix with other ingredients, except brandy. Press down lightly into earthenware jar and cover with brandy. Keep in cool place (below 57°F/14°C) and stir every few days.
   Keeps about 2 months.

SALADE SÉGUIN

Hot goat cheese salad. Recipe of Monsieur Mouret of the St-Hubert, Entrechaux.

For each person

2oz/50g ($\frac{1}{4}$ cup) smoked lean diced bacon
2 small slices bread, diced
1 small goat's cheese (not too hard)
1 tbs/15ml flour
$\frac{1}{2}$ egg
salt and pepper
1 tbs/15ml white breadcrumbs
2tbs/30ml olive oil
1 tsp/5ml wine vinegar
$\frac{1}{2}$ tsp/2.5ml made mustard
inner leaves of lettuce

Put bacon and bread together in a dish in medium-hot oven, so that fat from bacon is absorbed by the bread to form croûtons. Take out when all are golden.
   Roll cheese in flour, beaten and seasoned egg, then white breadcrumbs. This coating prevents it running while the centre becomes melting-soft. Put in pre-heated oven at 375°F/190°C/Gas Mark 5 for 6–7 minutes.
   Make up vinaigrette by placing oil, wine vinegar and mustard in a screw-top jar and shaking vigorously. Toss lettuce in vinaigrette.
   Place cheese carefully on lettuce, scatter crisp bacon pieces and croûtons around it and serve.

Salade Séguin

FRUITY DESSERTS

. . . . one breathed the plum's liquid freshness, the peach's flowing lymph; one breathed almond's milk and pear's juice; one breathed the maternal sap of orchards nourished by their own sugar. . . .
HENRI BOSCO, *SYLVIUS*

On the edge of the vineyard below our farmhouse stands an almond tree. In late February or early March its explosion of pink blossom reminds us of all the delicious things one can make with September's almonds. And all the other budding and blossoming about to burst on us in joyful abundance.

From May a succession of treats begins, bringing all the colours under the Provence sun. First, the red and white currants, and strawberries which continue for several months. Then cherries and raspberries all through June – with tiny wild strawberries if you know the right woods to find

Almond tree in flower, Visan

Figues fraîches aux framboises

them. July has almost everything at once: peaches, best eaten just as they are; glowing apricots to make a mousse with raspberries; nectarines and plums, golden or velvety blue; dark green water-melon with red flesh and black seeds, and pale green Cavaillon melon with rich orange flesh, so good with a little Beaumes-de-Venise and fresh mint; and the first crop of figs, growing more refreshingly succulent as the summer grows hotter.

At Châteaurenard market every northern Mediterranean fruit in every variety is to be found. Take peaches alone. From June onwards, the white peaches – for jams, sorbets, soufflés. Then as the summer gets hotter, the yellow peaches for preserves, tarts, beignets, and

garnishing of dishes. The market becomes more and more hectic. 'Wait till August,' said peach-and-plum grower, Monsieur Combe. 'It's crazy here. You can't move for produce – there are ten varieties of table grapes alone!'

We have three growing on our *tonnelle*, an arbour which provides natural shade for our terrace in high summer – black Hambourg Muscat, and white Chasselas and Italia. The birds prefer the Italia, and they're right. Luckily, long after the feathered survivors of the hunting season have migrated to Africa, grapes are still with us – till late autumn. In September, under a friend's huge fig tree, we have also enjoyed the Roger Vergé spectacular Chilled Fresh Figs with Raspberries: open three ripe figs per person, fill centre with raspberries and serve on a bed of whipped cream with *eau-de-vie de framboise* (raspberry liqueur).

Towards the end of September the almonds we dreamed about in March are bursting out of their thick green shells, and the wine harvesters are busy with the *vendange*. Pears and apples are at their best, so it's the time to make a potent pear-and-apple *compôte* with Visan red wine, or a pear tart with almonds.

It was partly the almonds that brought Jean-Michel Darros, pastry cook, to Provence. For he loves to use them in his recipes. After rigorous training at Lenôtre, the distinguished Paris pâtisserie, Jean-Michel grew tired of city life and headed south. In the gastronomy of the Mediter-

Fruit trees, Tulette

Pastrycook
Jean-Michel Darros,
Céreste

ranean, the gooey gâteau and sugary sweetmeat figure as large as the ladies who dote on them – from Tangier to Tel Aviv, from Istanbul to Barcelona. Not to mention the gentlemen. And Provence is no exception: just the place for a bright young pastrycook like Jean-Michel to begin a life of his own.

In the depths of wild, rolling countryside near Céreste, we found him re-inventing Provençal recipes. He had made himself a small workshop and living room by rebuilding a ruined peasant house. That day, helped by a shy, bespectacled young apprentice from Reillanne, Jean-Michel was using almonds as the basis of his tart called *Croquenbouche* (Munch-in-Mouth), which was also the name of his business.

'The one thing a pastrycook can't have,' said Jean-Michel, taking his partly-baked pastry shell, light as shortbread, out of the oven, 'is hot hands. Butter melts, sugar sticks. In July and August, I

have to cool mine on this marble slab.' Now it was the coolest surface to make an almond cream, with eggs, butter, ground almonds, rum and sugar. The cream went into the tart, and the tart back into the oven to finish cooking. I admired his cool temperament and cool hands; I would have freaked out with the complicated measurements. 'That's the secret of a pastrycook's success,' he said. 'You have to be precise with measurements and cooking times, or you'll have a disaster. Whereas in most other cooking, you can screw up things a little and still get by. That's why so many top chefs began as pastrycooks – it's the best training.'

But Provence can be a tough place for an outsider to start a business. A baker in Céreste had physically assaulted Jean-Michel, while he was setting up his stall in the village. 'He tore down my signs, then went about writing his own address on my business cards!' It was like a Pagnol play. Everyone in the village took sides, mostly – to the

Croquenbouche's stall,
Apt market

Kaki fruit tree, Tulette

credit of Céreste – championing Jean-Michel. He certainly found out who his friends were, and now has a loyal clientele of regulars.

Emotions are seldom mild in Provence – like the weather, they blow very hot or very cold. And when the chilly winter mistrals begin, frayed tempers are soothed by the last fruit of the year, the aromatic quince, stuffed and baked or made into *pâté*. The cherries we bottled in brandy during the summer bring on a benevolent glow in time for the great Provençal Christmas.

Strange that the part of France which has been fiercely anti-clerical ever since housing a foreign pope should recognise religious symbolism even in its Christmas eating habits. The Christmas Eve meatless *Gros Souper*, prior to Midnight Mass, begins with salt cod and ends traditionally with the Thirteen Desserts, representing Christ and the Twelve Apostles and having the delightful collective name of *pachichoio*.

Poor country people often found it difficult to make up the full thirteen. Generally they managed the obligatory *Pompe à l'huile* (sweet, flat pastry), and homemade nougat, making up as near the thirteen as possible from what was in the loft – apples, pears, grapes and a variety of dried fruit and nuts. So the spread varied from family to family, and still does. In the bourgeois homes of Marseilles, Port of the Orient, there would be oranges, mandarins, dates and other exotica. For the children, *papillottes*, little sweet crackers.

Yvonne Soliva of Le Moulin de Tante Yvonne, Lambesc, was one of those children over seventy years ago. Descended from a Marseillais count, she remembers those traditional Christmases with great affection: 'One never put the Infant Jesus in the crib before the pre-Mass supper, because he hadn't been born yet. I was woken up when my parents came back from Midnight Mass, so that I could put the baby in the crib.'

Then there was the festival of Candelmas in February. Little cakes in the shape of a boat called *Navettes de St-Victor* represented the boat in which the Saints Mary arrived from the Holy Land with their black servant, Sara, at Les Saintes-Marie-de-la-Mer in the Camargue. But what the young Yvonne Soliva liked best about that busy day was a more pagan custom. 'We used to make *crêpes*,

Lemon tree, Le Barroux

made *vin cuit*; 'cooked wine' certainly isn't a just translation but Lucien Peyraud gave us this vivid description of how it's made: The unfermented juice of the sweetest grapes, Grenache and Clairette, was boiled and reduced by a third in a big brass pot for five or six hours. Some poor kid had to watch over it, constantly stirring with a stick. Then it was poured into a bucket – and the kid kept stirring till his arm dropped off. By evening it had cooled off, and was put in the same uncleaned cask year after year.'Then wait for the miracle of fermentation. We've made it this way for fifty years. Some years it's awful, other years subtle and perfumed – like port. It's good for Christmas because, with only 10° alcohol, a new-born baby can safely drink it.'

Not so that grander Provençal dessert wine, Muscat de Beaumes-de-Venise, which can reach 15°, stronger than most sweet Bordeaux. The muscat grape was brought to Provence by that fourteenth-century poet, Good King Réné. And a later poet, Mistral, looking out towards Avignon from beneath those surreal jagged hills known as the Dentelles de Montmirail, wrote: 'The good Muscat de Beaumes and Wild Thyme Wine . . . you open your mouth and down they go, without the bottle touching your lips.'

I've never tasted Wild Thyme Wine; but a good Castaud Maurin Muscat de Beaumes-de-Venise goes down very smoothly with almost anything sweet.

clutching a gold piece in the hand which held the frying pan. Then we'd toss the coin up on to the top of the kitchen dresser and it had to stay there the whole year. It was supposed to stop us being short of money.'

With all festive sweetmeats went golden home-

NAVETTES DE ST-VICTOR

Saint Victor's boats. A traditional recipe.
Good accompaniment to many of our fruit desserts.
Serves 6–8.

1lb/450g (4 cups) sifted flour
9oz/250g (1 cup) sugar
2½oz/75g (¼ cup) butter
3 eggs
grated rind of 1 lemon
4 tbs/60ml water
4 tbs/60ml orange-flower water

TO FINISH

1 egg yolk
1 tbs/15ml milk

On working surface, knead all ingredients together and leave for 1 hour. Take little balls of mixture and form into ovals, with pointed ends. Flatten a little. Space out on oiled baking sheet. Slit each oval lightly longways with point of knife. This gives boat shape. Let dry for 2 hours.

Beat egg yolk in milk and brush over boats. Bake in moderate oven at 375°F/190°C/Gas Mark 5 until well puffed out and golden.

MELON DE CAVAILLON AU BEAUMES-DE-VENISE ET À LA MENTHE

The recipe for melon with Beaumes-de-Venise (aperitif made from muscat grapes) and mint is almost shorter than its title.

FOR EACH PERSON

half a ripe melon
2 tbs/30ml Beaumes-de-Venise aperitif
a few mint leaves

Take out the melon seeds and remove flesh with a melon-baller. Replace flesh in shell, pour over the aperitif, and decorate with mint leaves. Keep in the fridge until the moment of serving.

MOUSSE D'ABRICOTS AVEC UN COULIS DE FRAMBOISE

Apricot mousse with raspberry sauce. Serves 6.

1lb/450g apricots
2 tbs/30ml honey
5oz/150g ($\frac{1}{2}$ cup) caster (superfine) sugar
3 eggs
scant 1oz/25g (3tbs) cornflour
4 tbs/60ml water
$\frac{1}{4}$ pint/150ml ($\frac{2}{3}$ cup) double (heavy) cream

RASPBERRY SAUCE

10oz/300g fresh raspberries
1 tbs/15ml honey
1 tbs/15ml water

Wash apricots and remove stones (pits). Cook gently with 1 tbs/15ml water, 2 tbs/30ml honey and half the caster sugar for 15 minutes. Blend in mixer.

Separate yolks from whites of eggs; beat yolks with the rest of the sugar until creamy, then add cornflour mixed with 3 tbs/45ml water. Mix well with apricot purée and heat gently in a thick casserole, lifting mixture off the bottom all the time with a spatula. Take off heat as first bubbles appear and mixture thickens up. Beat egg whites till stiff. Turn into mixture, which must be very hot, and beat energetically. Cool and refrigerate. Decorate with cream.

Put aside some of the biggest raspberries to decorate the mousse. To make the sauce, heat the rest of the fruit with 1 tbs honey and 1 tbs water until the juice runs. Break up the fruit, then put through a sieve. Refrigerate before serving with the mousse.

TARTE AU CITRON ET AUX AMANDES

Lemon tart with almonds. Serves 6.

FILLING

2 eggs
4$\frac{1}{2}$oz/125g ($\frac{1}{2}$ cup) sugar
1$\frac{1}{2}$ lemons, grated rind and juice
4$\frac{1}{2}$oz/125g ($\frac{1}{2}$ cup) butter
2oz/50g ($\frac{1}{2}$ cup) ground almonds
1oz/25g (1$\frac{1}{2}$ tbs) whole blanched almonds

To make the pastry, follow the recipe for the pear tart with almonds.

For the filling, beat eggs and sugar until light and creamy. Mix in lemon rind and juice, then melted butter and ground almonds. Pour into partly cooked pastry shell, put whole almonds on top and finish tart in oven at 375°F/190°C/Gas Mark 5 for 30 minutes or until set and golden. Both these tarts are delicious eaten slightly warm with cream.

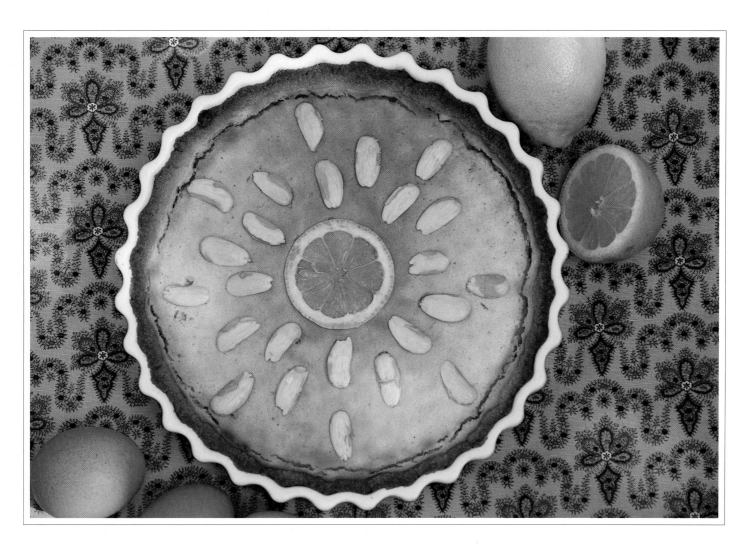

Tarte au citron et aux amandes

TARTE AUX POIRES ET AUX AMANDES

Pear tart with almonds. Serves 6.

SWEET SHORT PASTRY

2 eggs
3½oz/100g (½ cup) sugar
pinch of salt
7oz/200g (1½ cups) sifted flour
4½oz/125g (½ cup) butter
dried haricot beans

FILLING

4½oz/125g (½ cup) butter
4½oz/125g (½ cup) sugar
2 eggs
1oz/25g (2 tbs) flour
3½oz/100g (⅔ cup) ground almonds
few drops vanilla extract
2 large ripe pears
2oz/50g (3 tbs) whole almonds, lightly toasted

For the pastry, beat together eggs, sugar, and salt. Add flour in small amounts and mix well. Turn on to work surface, work in the cut-up butter with hands, until absorbed. Roll into ball and leave 1 hour in fridge. Roll out on lightly floured surface, line a 12in/30cm flan tin (tart pan) with pastry. Cut foil to cover bottom pastry and fill with beans to weight evenly for baking. Bake in medium oven at 400°F/200°C/Gas Mark 6 for 15 minutes, until firm but not cooked. Let shell cool slightly.

To make the filling, mix together butter, sugar, eggs, flour, ground almonds and vanilla. Peel pears, cut in half longways, lift out cores. Cut each half in slices, keeping pear shape, and place on pastry. Cover with almond cream, pressing toasted almonds between the pears.

Finish tart in moderately hot oven, 400°F/200°C/Gas Mark 6, until golden.

COINGS FARCIS AU FOUR

Baked stuffed quinces. Our recipe. Serves 4.

4 quinces
12 cloves
4 tbs/60ml honey, lavender or acacia
½ pint/300ml (1¼ cups) single (pouring) cream
2 handfuls pine-nuts
2 handfuls raisins
good pinch cinnamon
4fl oz/100ml (½ cup) white wine
4fl oz/100ml (½ cup) water

Peel the quinces and remove cores, leaving the base of the fruit intact. Push 3 cloves into each quince. Mix together honey, cream, pine-nuts, raisins and cinnamon. Spoon into the quinces, putting remainder of stuffing with wine and water around the quinces in a thick oven dish.

Bake at 400°F/200°C/Gas Mark 6 until quinces are a rich terracotta colour. Serve with cream.

Tarte aux poires et aux amandes

CRÈME D'AMANDES PARFUMÉE AU KIRSCH

Almond cream with Kirsch. A delicious recipe from Madame
Soliva of Le Moulin de Tante Yvonne, Lambesc.
Serves 10–12.

4–5 squares dark chocolate
9oz/250g (1⅛ cups) butter
5 eggs
grated rind of ½ lemon
9oz/250g (1⅛ cups) caster sugar
9oz/250g (2¼ cups) ground almonds
3 tbs/45ml Kirsch
sulphurized paper

Cut sulphurized paper to fit bottom and sides of a plastic container about 8in/20cm long by 4in/10cm wide and 2½in/6cm deep. Melt chocolate gently with 1 tsp/5ml water, and with a pastry brush, paint the paper with chocolate. When dry, replace paper in container.

In a bowl big enough to hold all the ingredients, beat the butter to a cream. In another bowl, beat together the eggs and the zest of lemon (use a wire 'balloon' whisk).

In a flame-proof casserole, or heavy pan, heat the sugar with 6 tbs/100 ml water and bring to a boil, stirring often. After 2 or 3 minutes, test by putting a drop of sugar in a saucer of cold water. Roll it between thumb and finger. When it makes a soft, fudgy ball, it is ready. Take off heat immediately. (Before this, it will be increasingly gluey.)

Whisking all the time, pour the boiling sugar into the egg mixture. Place bowl over bain-marie (pan of boiling water) and continue to whisk. When you lift the whisk and the mixture falls in a supple thread that doesn't break, yet is light in texture and a pale colour, take the bowl out of the bain-marie. Keep on beating (over cold water for speed) until the mixture is cool.

Add ground almonds and Kirsch to the butter in the bigger bowl, and beat together with hand-held electric beater. Still beating, add the cooled egg and sugar mixture. Beat for 4 or 5 minutes more to amalgamate the ingredients completely. Pour into the prepared chocolate-lined container and put into the deep-freeze to set.

An hour or so before serving, put into the fridge. Then turn out, peel off sulphurized paper, leaving coating of chocolate on the finished dessert (this needs care). Cut into slices about ¾in/1½cm thick and serve on individual dishes. This poem of a dish should not have any sauce or cream to mask the flavour.

COMPÔTE DU VIEUX VIGNERON

Old vinegrower's stewed fruit. This folksy literal translation does at least place the recipe; it comes from the vineyards of the Côtes-du-Rhône. Serves 6.

juice of 1 orange
12oz/350g (1½ cups) sugar
2lb/900g apples
1oz/30g/2 tbs butter
¾ bottle Côtes-du-Rhône (or full-bodied red wine)
1 clove
pinch of ginger
6 perfect pears

Put orange juice and half sugar in heavy pan and cook to a syrup. Peel and core apples, cut up and cook in syrup till soft. Process or blend to purée. Return to pan and add butter, stirring over a low heat. Turn into a deep serving dish.

Mix wine with rest of sugar, clove and ginger. Heat and boil for 3–4 minutes. Peel pears, cut in halves longways and lift out cores. Put pears in boiling wine, and simmer until they are translucent. Drain and place in star shape on apple purée.

Reduce wine by boiling until it is very syrupy. Take out clove; pour syrup over the compote. Serve just warm or very cold.

CERISES À L'EAU-DE-VIE

Cherries in brandy. These take six weeks to mature and will keep a long time – if they get the chance. Serve each person with 5 or 6 cherries with a little of their liquor, in a small glass with a spoon, after the meal when coffee is served.

1lb/450g ripe cherries
1¾ pints/1 litre (4½ cups) alcohol or brandy (40%)
1 stick cinnamon
a few coriander seeds
¾lb/350g perfect whole cherries
4oz/110g (½ cup) sugar

Crush the ripe cherries, smash the stones (seeds) of half of them, and put in a jar with alcohol or brandy, cinnamon and coriander seeds. Cover and leave in a warm place for 15 days. Strain off liquid into another jar. Throw away the cherry pulp. Fill jar with perfect whole cherries, cutting their stalks to half length. Add sugar. Cover and leave for 1 month in sun, turning the other way up every day.

MORE SWEET THINGS

Its weight is such that the wood of those trees,
dried up by the sun and wind, often splits apart and the
honey is shed, while the fury of millions of bees sets
the sky ablaze.
JEAN GIONO, 'ENNEMONDE'

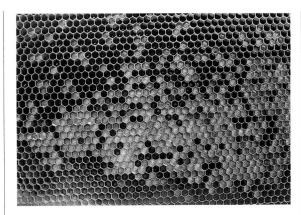

No wonder they were angry. It was a tough life being a bee. 'A honey-maker loves his bees,' said André Augier, 'but he exploits them without pity.' The hive we were about to inspect contained fifty thousand bees with a life expectancy of one month. If they had been born in October they could make it through the winter by hibernating; but the longer the life, the duller.

Monsieur Augier pumped the small bellows, and a heady aroma of pine-needle smoke

Lavender field, Taulignan

André Augier calms
his bees with smoke

engulfed the heavy frame he had lifted from the hive. I was glad of my helmet; though the smoke did have its calming effect on the bees, thick as a rush-hour crowd upon golden wax cells. I winced, as he nimbly picked one up between finger and thumb. 'The males are too lazy to sting,' he assured me. 'There's a few hundred of these drones, and one queen. The queen lasts five years, but when a drone is no more use to her, she liquidates him.'

He put the drone down for the queen to have her way with, whatever it might be, and turned the frame towards the setting sun. The light turned the golden comb transparent. Delicious nectar dripped from the frame on to the hive's lid. We sniffed and tasted, and decided the 1987 had more than a hint of lavender in its bouquet. And Monsieur Augier decided the honey was ready to be collected. 'It's amusing work, really rewarding when you see hives full of honey like these. Easy work, too – if you're strong enough to lift the frames!' I couldn't even shift them, let alone lift; but the honey-filled frames, beneath shade-giving oak trees in a disused truffle-oak plantation, would now be lifted off the base by strong men, and transported to Augier's headquarters in Vaison-la-Romaine for processing into jars.

For rights to let his bees 'graze' on a farmer's lavender, he paid one kilo of honey per hive. Fields between Taulignan and Grignan dazzled us in the light of the magic evening hour. Bright, rain-fed lavender meant good and plentiful honey, so Monsieur Augier got back into his large, comfortable Citroën Pallas in a very good mood.

Monsieur Augier was a big honey man, we gathered, his hives extending all over: Vaucluse for lavender honey; the Drôme for acacia honey; the Alpilles for rosemary honey; and Haute-Pro-

André Boyer, nougat maker

André Boyer's nougat shop, Sault

So all was not always sweetness and light in Provence – even for a purveyor of honey to the grandest London stores. Back at Vaison, Augier proudly showed us labels printed 'Lavender Honey from Mont Ventoux, specially packed for Fortnum & Mason'. Another British firm marketed Royal Jelly, the by-product of honey said to be a sexual stimulant, with the slogan 'Bees do it'.

For anyone preferring honey in other forms, sweet-toothed Provence is the place to find them. The word 'Nougat' on signs every few yards of Montélimar's long, dead straight southern approaches (they resemble the worst of Los Angeles) proclaim it to be the Nougat Capital of the Western Hemisphere. Those who love nougat – and they are many, judging by Montélimar's honey-voiced hype – should go to Sault, a charming small town, surrounded by lavender fields. Set high on the Plateau de Vaucluse, Sault rejoices in

vence for pine honey. Although normally people were too afraid of being stung to meddle with his unguarded hives (peasants used to keep their *Louis d'Or* coins in theirs!), he had had his share of villainy. Once he found all upturned, the bees gone. A jealous peasant who had wished to buy the land was suspected, and questioned by the police. Nothing could be proved, but later the peasant was found dead on André Augier's land in somewhat mysterious circumstances. 'Very embarrassing,' said Monsieur Augier with a wry smile, continuing quickly: 'Then there was the lawyer who made a mistake in the contract for a piece of land I'd bought. He forgot to mention one lot, and the old lady sold it again – to someone else! When I tried to claim it, she said something I wouldn't repeat in front of your daughter. So I said: "That won't get you to Paradise, *ma belle!*" and she replied: "So what? I don't believe in Paradise."'

Lombardi's shop, Aix-en-Provence

153

André Rastouil making
crystallized fruit, Gargas

flat country for walkers, forest trails for riders, panoramas for painters, and wild flowers for botanists. And André Boyer for nougat addicts. His shop in the centre of town is the meeting-place for visiting dignitaries.

'Let me present the Mayor of Simiane,' said Monsieur Boyer, our host, popping a champagne cork in honour of the neighbouring mayor. It was time for the eleven o'clock glass, Boyer entertaining in style after the morning's nougat-making, which had begun at five. Talk was of his centenary celebrations; great grandfather Ernest Boyer, a Sault pâtissier, had started the business in 1887.

'Call us artisanal – forget that industrial stuff from you-know-where,' he laughed. 'We use lavender honey and almonds grown round Sault. And the very purest and most natural bourbon vanilla.'

Behind the shop was the kitchen with fine old Provençal furniture where Boyer entertained; and behind that the packing room where his mother and wife wrapped slabs of nougat in cellophane and stuck on labels, aided by his small sons aged four and six. And in the workshop were his black assistant and his chef, André Gaillard – keeper of a thousand secrets.

I asked if a few could be revealed. Boyer showed us his *torrefacteur*, an ancient oven for grilling almonds. 'If they're too grilled or the sugar's not crystallized enough, we chuck 'em away. No regrets. Quality's the best publicity.'

So it seems there is really not too much to nougat-making, if you don't mind burning your fingers. Black nougat is cooked fast; it is crisp and caramel-tasting. White nougat is cooked slowly in a *bain-marie*; it is soft and honey-tasting. For a simple home-made nougat, pour lavender honey into a heavy-based pan, bring it to the boil, constantly stirring. Add an equal weight of whole almonds (with skins left on). Continue to cook and stir till honey darkens and almonds crack. Take pan off heat and go on stirring for ten minutes. Turn out mixture into rectangular pan lined with rice-paper, and put more rice-paper on top. Let it cool and cut into bars.

Crystallized mandarin oranges and plums

Rather harder to make (and not worth the trouble if you happen to be in the neighbourhood of Aix-en-Provence) are Calissons d'Aix. These delicious little sweetmeats contain whole almonds, crystallized melon, lavender honey and orange-flower water. When we visited one of the town's most famous *confiseries*, they were reluctant to let us photograph the workshop. But I did manage to get a glimpse, through a grille at pavement level, of workers at their benches; it looked positively Dickensian in there. The dark and stuffy basement bore no relation to the shop's light, elegant interior.

Crystallized melons for Calissons d'Aix are made at the Confiserie St-Denis, Gargas, near Apt. Here another André (Rastouil) has his little factory, full of brilliant fruits simmering in black cauldrons. For a time, he had tried commercial production of crystallized fruit but returned to the old artisanal method.

'Gargas is right at the hub of fruit production,' Monsieur Rastouil told us. 'I get melons from Cavaillon; apricots from Salons; peaches from the Gard; figs from Salernes; pears from Digne; clementines from Corsica; and plums from around here.'

We followed clementines through various stages of crystallization. Each clementine is pricked to let sugar enter. Blanched for several hours. Soaked in steam-prepared syrup for twenty-four hours. Then, for about seven weeks, the soaking-in-syrup process is repeated, each time the syrup becoming a little stronger as it takes the humidity out of the fruit and feeds it sugar. Finally comes the intensive work of glazing the fruit, a delicate manual operation.

Two-thirds of Monsieur Rastouil's trade occurs at the Christmas rush. But during the tourist season, it is worthwhile for Madame Rastouil to run a small artisanal shop. As well as their own crystallized fruits, the shop sells Provençal sugar dolls, dried fruit much favoured by British visitors to put in Christmas cakes, and goat's cheeses made of almond paste for practical jokes.

*If I were king, I would close all cafés, for those who
frequent them become dangerous hotheads.*
CHARLES DE MONTESQUIEU

Provence offers many pleasant ways of finishing a meal, from collapsing contentedly into a hammock to working up an appetite for the next by a country walk, stick at the ready to swipe the all-too-frequent farm dog snapping at your heels. But between the supine and the energetic, I would settle for a coffee on the Cours Mirabeau, Aix-en-Provence.

The café, of course, would be Les Deux Garçons, that fin-de-siècle miracle of mirrors and lamps and waiters dressed as though about to serve their two local boys, Paul Cézanne and Emile Zola. Arguably France's most beautiful main street, the elegant eighteenth century Cours Mirabeau is known, to the fury of the sophisticated Aixois, as the Champs Elysées of Provence.

As I sat, sipping my expresso – a good, strong Italianate taste in Provence's most Tuscan town, I reflected on what a fine spectacle a few francs can buy on the terrace of a southern café. Over to my left, the statue of good King René holding a bunch of the muscat grapes he introduced to France. Besides his talent as working vineyard owner, this truly Renaissance figure was mathematician, geo-

Les Deux Garçons,
Aix-en-Provence

logist, musician, and poet; in his reign both St-Sauveur cathedral and the University were completed.

King René's spirit lives on in the town's 36% student population, half of them foreigners, and there was a youthful buzz about the clientèle of Les Deux Garçons that afternoon. '*Auriez-vous un franc, M'sieur?*' a raven-haired, olive-skinned girl asked me, as she table-hopped. The conditional tense when begging? How polite, I thought. Till I discovered she was not on the scrounge for coffee money, but collecting energetically for a student charity.

Watching the students go stylishly by on the Cours Mirabeau, I was glad to see them stop at Les Deux Garçons. Expensive restaurants would be beyond the means of most, Provençal gastronomy the stuff of glossy magazines. Yet here they were able to indulge in that most convivial of Provençal pursuits – meeting at a café to plan a revolution or a seduction.

Alas, it is not always so leisurely. Inevitably, Le Fast Food has become the latest invader in Provence's history of foreign influences. Take Avignon, for instance. Across the road from one another, two hamburger hells compete for trade in the rue de la République, the city's main drag.

We were there for the Theatre Festival. Groups of young actors in garish make-up, like medieval mountebanks, handed out leaflets announcing their shows to the Fast Fooders. White-faced clowns and chantilly cream, gaudy cheeks and technicolour jello seemed to fuse in an infantile dream of Anglo-Saxon treats, soft-option consumption at no special time of day or night – for children of all ages. And nationalities – including the French.

I am the first to enjoy a good hamburger in New York. But in Provence, where Le Slow Food is our joy, the sheer speed of service and consumption seemed aggressively urban. Like the bad-

Pizza van, Apt

Baronne de Waldner's
herb garden, Le Barroux

tempered Avignon café waitress who sneeringly dismissed our complaints about olives like withered testicles, and answered Carey's fluent, if heavily accented French, with a special brand of mean-sounding, execrable English beloved of the French tourist trade.

Like electric pylons striding brutishly across garrigues, and like missiles pointing at Moscow from the Plateau de Vaucluse, Le Fast Food is symptomatic of the worst of progress. In this book we have tried to portray, as well as the pleasures, the twilight of a certain naturalness of Provençal life, mirrored elsewhere in France.

But trends come and fashions go. Nouvelle Cuisine, which could be charitably described as less food on larger plates for more money – a bird's dropping of polenta, a daub of raspberry *coulis* – has at least left us the happy legacy of its beauty of presentation. And Provençal chefs have absorbed and developed this. But finally it is the land that counts, the land that produces. Young chefs like Jany Gleize remain loyal to their *terroir* rather than desert it for some temple of French gastronomy in Los Angeles. And, despite the international stardom of a whole new generation of French chefs, I do not see Jean-André Charial as the first gastronaut, serving his *Gigot d'agneau en croûte* on Mars.

The scene may be changing, but we can still linger over a coffee on the Cours Mirabeau. Or for those who prefer something less stimulating but still spurn *le décaf*, try a soothing herb *tisane* from the many suggested in Maurice Messegué's book *Mon Herbier de Santé*. Most plants and aromatic herbs are available in Provence: perhaps an infusion of verbena from the harvest of the Boeuf granddaughter, Chantal; or dried lime-flowers from Vaison-la-Romaine market; or more or less anything from the Elizabethan-style herb garden of Baronne Lulu de Waldner at Le Barroux.

Not forgetting herbs in a stronger form, provided by Brother Gérard in the monks' famous Aiguebelle liqueur. As to whether this *digestif* aids the digestion or not, I could not swear; it certainly sends one out singing.

So as I drain my last drop of coffee on the Cours Mirabeau, no post-prandial melancholy descends. The scene may be changing, but the tastes of Provence, in their infinite variety, seem inexhaustible. And tomorrow is another feast day.

Winter sunrise in the hills of Provence

159

ACKNOWLEDGEMENTS

Our thanks are due to the following, who have helped us in all kinds
of ways to discover the many tastes of Provence:

Claude Arnaud, Albert Astier, André Augier, Paul Avril, Kinou and
Françoise Bartheye, Monsieur Bernard, Julien and Lucienne Boeuf and Chantal,
Michel Bosc, André Boyer, Georges and Catherine Brunet, Jean-André Charial,
Louis Chauvet, Monsieur Combe, Confrérie de Saint-Vincent,
Monsieur Copiatti, Quentin Crewe, Jean-Michel Darros, Madame Dijour,
Jean-Claude Dumas, Docteur Bernard Ely, Marie-Anne and Florent Founès,
Brother Gérard, Jean and Mady Gilardi, Pierre, Arlette, and Jany Gleize,
Monsieur and Madame Georges Gugliemenetti, Guy Jullien, Monsieur and Madame
Leon Laget, Monsieur Lantelme, Nadine Latour, Chanet Le Franc,
Messrs Leroy and Berger, Monsieur Llorens, Jenny and Peter Mayle,
Charles Mouret, Monsieur and Madame Ollivier, Monsieur and Madame Ordener,
Lucien and Lucienne Peyraud, Monsieur J. Ramade, Pierrot, Lili and Pierre
Ramour, Monsieur and Madame André Rastouil, Monsieur Rippert, Madame Roux,
Francis Sack, Yvonne and André Soliva, Steven Spurrier, Raymond Thuilier,
Max Veron, Baronne Lulu de Waldner, Timmy Johnston.

Thanks for permission to reprint are due to:

The Marcel Pagnol Estate
From *Fanny* © Fasquelle 1932, by Marcel Pagnol

The Colette Estate
From *Letters* (letter to Francis Poulenc) © Flammarion 1958, by Colette.

Gallimard
From *Rondeur des Jours* (Provence) © Gallimard 1943, by Jean Giono.
From *Ennémonde* © Gallimard 1968 and Peter Owen Ltd, UK, by Jean Giono.
From *Sylvius* © Gallimard 1970, by Henri Bosco.

'L'Elixir du Révérend Père Gaucher' and 'La Chèvre de Monsieur
Séguin' are from *Lettres de Mon Moulin* by Alphonse Daudet.